SNAKES AND LADDERS

Snakes and Ladders

A PERSONAL EXPLORATION OF QUAKER WORK
ON HUMAN RIGHTS AT THE UNITED NATIONS

Rachel Brett

THE 2012 SWARTHMORE LECTURE

First published May 2012

Quaker Books, Friends House, 173 Euston Road, London NW1 2BJ

www.quaker.org.uk

978-1-907123-26-9

© Rachel Brett 2012

Cover Photo: Nick Southall – http://www.flickr.com/people/njsouthall

'The Gate of the Year' by Minnie Louise Haskins.
© Minnie Louise Haskins, 1908.
Reproduced by permission of Sheil Land Associates Ltd.

Book designed and typeset by: Cox Design, Witney

Printed by: Information Press

FSC
www.fsc.org
MIX
Paper from
responsible sources
FSC® C013262

THE SWARTHMORE LECTURE

The Swarthmore lectureship was established by the Woodbrooke Extension Committee at a meeting held 9 December 1907: the minute of the committee providing for an "annual lecture on some subject relating to the message and work of the Society of Friends". The name Swarthmore was chosen in memory of the home of Margaret Fox, which was always open to the earnest seeker after Truth, and from which loving words of sympathy and substantial material help were sent to fellow workers.

The lectureship continues to be under the care of Woodbrooke Quaker Study Centre Trustees, and is a significant part of the education work undertaken at and from Woodbrooke.

The lectureship has a twofold purpose: first, to interpret to the members of the Society of Friends their message and mission; and second, to bring before the public the spirit, aims and fundamental principles of Friends. The lecturers alone are responsible for any opinions expressed.

The lectureship provides both for the publication of a book and for the delivery of a lecture, the latter usually at the time of Britain Yearly Meeting of the Society of Friends. A lecture related to the present book was delivered at Yearly Meeting in London on the evening of Saturday 26 May 2012.

The Swarthmore Lecture Committee can be contacted via the Clerk, c/o Woodbrooke Quaker Study Centre, 1046 Bristol Road, Selly Oak, Birmingham B29 6LJ.

Woodbrooke
Quaker Study Centre

QUAKERS

CONTENTS

PREFACE

This is an attempt to distil and reflect on my many years of experience of working on human rights and refugees issues for the Religious Society of Friends (Quakers) at their Offices to the United Nations, in particular at the Quaker UN Office (QUNO) in Geneva.

I first discovered the Quaker work at the UN when, in 1976, I became the Administrative Assistant to J. Duncan Wood, the Director of QUNO Geneva. At that time, this was a post for a Young Friend and was the precursor to the current Programme Assistant position. Becoming convinced that this Quaker work was for me, in 1978 I became an intern with QUNO New York, working on human rights with Gordon M. Browne Jr. During that year I was involved in drafting and negotiating through the UN General Assembly resolution 33/165, commonly referred to as the CO/apartheid resolution because it gave quasi-refugee status to those fleeing South Africa because of their refusal to serve in military or police forces being used to enforce apartheid. In order to qualify better for the Quaker work on human rights, I then gained a degree in law, followed later by a Masters degree in International Human Rights Law. In 1993, I returned to QUNO Geneva to take up the human rights work.

To the extent that this is a personal narrative, it must be clearly understood that QUNO, and I, were usually only acting as one player amongst many and, therefore, nothing written here should be interpreted as claims to special powers or achievements. In particular, many pieces of work were initiated by previous QUNO staff and were done in conjunction with others. Furthermore, many of these reflections are based on 'lessons learned' in the sense of what did not happen, or what might have been done better, rather than of successes.

At the same time, as requested by the Swarthmore Lecture Committee, this is a set of personal reflections and stories, not a researched analysis, of why Quakers work on human rights issues at the United Nations and how they do it. As such it is a witness to the human rights work of QUNO to which is added some historical background in order to provide a context for the Quaker UN work and for some of the issues.

Why "Snakes and Ladders"? This well known children's board game entails trying to move up the board from start to finish.

Landing at the bottom of a ladder provides a boost, while landing on the head of a snake slides the player back down the board. A similar game is known in other cultures, and probably originated as a spiritual teaching tool in India.

I used this title for my report on the 58th session of the UN Commission on Human Rights (2002) to highlight the unpredictable element in working with political human rights bodies at the UN, combined with the importance of keeping trying. This was the time when many of the seemingly assured fundamentals of human rights, such as the prohibition on torture, were being questioned in the wake of the 9/11 attacks. At such times, it becomes even clearer that unless we continue to 'go round the board' we abdicate our responsibility to try to move forward or, at the worst, maintain the *status quo* and resist regression. Much the same is true of Quaker work at the UN in general: being willing to start again in face of setbacks, and being available to take advantage of the ladders when we find them, but above all having clarity of vision, creativity in finding different approaches, and persistence.

Particular thanks go to my link Friends on the Swarthmore Lecture Committee, Shelagh Robinson and Douglas Rennie, and to my support group comprised of Martin Macpherson, Jonathan Woolley and my family. Special appreciation goes to Peggy Brett, including for her insight about and drawing of the intelligent, friendly and supportive FWCC octopus.

This Lecture is dedicated to all those who have walked this road with me – as mentors, as companions, as fellow toilers in the vineyard and as friends, but above all to my family (in alphabetical order to prevent arguments), Derek, Edward, Jennifer and Peggy, but for whom the work this Lecture draws on would have been impossible.

ABBREVIATIONS

AFSC	American Friends Service Committee
BYM	Britain Yearly Meeting
CFSC	Canadian Friends Service Committee
FWCC	Friends World Committee for Consultation
HSN	Human Security Network
IDP	internally displaced person
ILO	International Labour Organisation
NGO	non-governmental organisation
OSCE	Organisation for Security and Cooperation in Europe
QAAC	[Canadian] Quaker Aboriginal Affairs Committee
QCEA	Quaker Council for European Affairs
QPSW	Quaker Peace and Social Witness
QUNC	Quaker United Nations Committee
QUNO	Quaker United Nations Office
UNHCR	United Nations High Commissioner for Refugees
WHO	World Health Organisation
WTO	World Trade Organisation

CHAPTER 1

Introduction

*What doth the Lord require of thee, but to do justly,
and to love mercy, and to walk humbly with thy God?*

(Micah 6:8)

Peace, justice and the fact that there is something of God in everyone – hence our approach to people and non-discrimination of all kinds – are for me the touchstones of living our Quaker values.[1] To work *as a Quaker* – not merely *for Quakers* – is a real challenge. It means that you have to be prepared for your actions (or inaction) and attitudes to be measured against Quaker beliefs and testimonies. Others may from time to time be able to be anonymous ('normal' people), but to be visibly a Quaker means that Quakers are judged by you. It is an enormous responsibility – and one which it is, of course, impossible to live up to. It therefore also requires the practice of Quaker understanding and forgiveness for your own inability to attain perfection or even maintain an approximation of it.

What does this mean to me in terms of my work as a Quaker at the United Nations (UN)? First, it is what drove me to this work. Quakers have a particular contribution to make as a non-governmental organisation (NGO) in consultative status with the UN.[2] This includes the willingness not to divide countries, any more than individuals, into the 'good' and the 'bad' but to be willing to meet with and listen to all: to hear what contributions each has to make, without losing our own principles and integrity in the process, without being confrontational or antagonistic, which does not necessarily mean letting things with which we disagree go unchallenged.

Second, we are able to organise meetings between people who would not otherwise meet, or which if organised by others, particularly by a government, would be perceived (whether or not correctly) as being biased or having a hidden agenda. This is both because of our non-confrontational (but constructively critical) attitude to *all* and because of our historical involvement at the UN and in humanitarian work. A particular aspect of this is the relatively long time that Quaker representatives stay in post compared with the three-, four- or five-year rotation of diplomats, as well as our recognised expertise in the issues, and 'neutrality' in political terms (though not on moral issues). Because of these, we are often sought out as sources of information, expertise and ideas.

This is clearly helped by our commitment to maintaining confidentiality when so requested, so that personal discussions are not disclosed. We are trusted not to breach confidence but also to be honest in our opinions – we will not say that we agree with someone or that we think their proposed course of action is a good one, if we do not think so. This means that often people prize our views and our good opinion. They want our approval. This can be seen as flattering, but it can also be problematic when we do not agree or approve!

Third, we recognise that we are dealing with *individuals* even when they represent a government, and that the individual may not fully agree with government policy and may be seeking to change it from within. At times I have found myself in the delightfully ironic position of writing references for representatives seeking to escape from government employment while simultaneously I was trying to change their government policy on one of 'our' issues. We can, therefore, maintain 'friendly relations' with representatives of governments with whose policies and behaviours we may profoundly disagree. However, most governments' policies and actions are not uniformly good or bad. So we may find ourselves working constructively on some issues with a government even while they are committing serious human rights violations or are engaged in an armed conflict.

To undertake this Quaker work is not easy: there are many dilemmas. To engage with the issues which face government representatives and those working in international organisations is to be constantly challenged to apply our Quaker beliefs to the real world in all its complexity. Sometimes we have to accept that we do not have 'solutions' in the short-term *realpolitik* sense. The issues on which we work are rarely 'popular' with either governments or other non-governmental organisations. Sometimes results are obvious but often we work for years with no apparent progress. To be able to continue working in this way requires belief in the rightness of what we are doing and that the work does reflect Quaker concerns and is, therefore, supported by Friends. How can we be sure that the course we pursue is right? Only by constantly seeking and testing our work and our methods through Quaker processes; by checking that our beliefs, integrity and concerns are not being subverted by others (or ourselves); by remaining true to our Quaker vision of a world without war and injustice, and the steps which lead in that direction.

Our methods of work are often misunderstood, particularly by other non-governmental organisations working on human rights issues. They tend to think we should take a public stand against the human rights abuses committed by one government or another and we often get lobbied to do so. It is hard for a local activist or victim of a human rights violation to accept that however much we may sympathise, we will not publicly berate their government (with the very limited and specific exceptions set out below), nor can we take up individual cases. Even Friends sometimes ask QUNO to denounce human rights violations in countries other than their own.

This used to be much more of a problem; but developing a clear articulation of why we take this position has helped, at least with the international NGOs and our regular interlocutors. This position derives from the nature of our organisation: there are Quakers living in many countries. Many governments are extremely unhappy to be publicly accused of human rights violations, and in these circumstances it would be the Quakers in that country who would be likely to suffer. If the representative Quaker body in a country asks QUNO to raise the human rights situation in their country, then we would expect to do so (subject to capacity and in the absence of specific other constraints). This might mean taking a public stance, or using our UN and government contacts to quietly inform and request action from them, depending on the circumstances and our judgement of likely effectiveness. Where there are 'external' Quaker actors/workers but no local Quakers, then the request for action would need to come from the responsible Quaker body such as the relevant Quaker service committee.

At the same time, the relations of trust we have developed with other international NGOs, combined with the recognition of the benefits of our approach at least in some circumstances, has contributed to better understanding. More recently, this has often led to such NGOs asking us to do our 'Quaker thing' (such as organise an informal, off-the-record lunch discussion) rather than expecting us to do the same kind of public advocacy that they do.

Finally, although many Friends and others value as quintessentially Quaker our informal, off-the-record meetings, we cannot do these unless we are visible and engaged with the diplomatic and other personnel and with the issues. It is essential to keep both a QUNO and an individual profile that is sufficiently known and recognised. It is the contacts with the people and the knowledge of the UN, the processes and the issues which enable us to convene our meetings and engage with the issues – at a minimum at the level of asking the right questions, although our insight and experiences are often key.[3]

CHAPTER 2

Why Quakers work on human rights issues

Everyone is entitled to all the rights and freedoms set forth in this Declaration, without distinction of any kind, such as race, colour, sex, language, religion, political or other opinion, national or social origin, property, birth or other status.

(Universal Declaration of Human Rights, 1948, Article 2.1)

I am a Quaker and a human rights lawyer. Therefore, it is perhaps my own bias and limitation that makes it seem to me self-evident that Quakers should be doing human rights work. Central to Quakerism as I understand it is the belief of "that of God" in every individual. For me, this leads essentially to the obligation that all should be treated as human beings with dignity and rights with its corollary that no-one should be dehumanised or stigmatised by labelling, whatever they may have done.[1]

Quakers may have thought about, or articulated, the issues on which they worked and continue to work, not as 'human rights' but, for example, as liberty, social welfare, social justice or penal reform. Nevertheless, the quintessential nature and the motivation can often be identified and phrased in human rights terms. In the case of work with and for refugees, for instance, it was probably seen as an expression of common humanity, humanitarian assistance, or giving succour to the stranger in our midst. Although current discourse, correctly, distinguishes a rights-based approach from a welfare one, they are not always so far apart in essence, though charity (in the general sense) can be patronising and have as much to do with the giver as the recipient, whereas human rights is about entitlements and being able to claim them.

A few historical examples

Pennsylvania was given to William Penn by Charles II in 1681 as repayment of a debt owed to his father; Penn established it as a state with liberty of conscience as an entrenched provision in its charter.

Adam Hochschild[2] describes the campaign for the abolition of the slave trade as "the greatest of all human rights movements" and identifies not only the central role of Quakers in starting and maintaining it, but also other continuing facets of Quaker human rights work, such as bringing in others who would carry more weight with the Establishment and letting them (in particular Wilberforce and Clarkson) take much of the credit. The 1688 Germantown Quaker Petition Against Slavery was the first protest against African American slavery made by a religious body in the English colonies, although it was not acted upon by the Quaker bodies to whom it was sent. In 1772 John

Woolman spoke at London Yearly Meeting, but action was delayed until 1783 when a petition was sent to Parliament. The call for abolition of slavery itself came later, although in 1776 Philadelphia Yearly Meeting prohibited members from owning slaves and as early as 1786 a group of Philadelphia Quakers had been noted as trying to help an escaped slave. Friends became prominent in the Underground Railroad helping escaping slaves to reach freedom, and on 11 February 1790, Friends petitioned the US Congress for the abolition of slavery.

John Bellers (1654–1725) argued for the complete abolition of capital punishment.[3] Originally, other Friends took a more limited approach, but from 1818 British Friends (London Yearly Meeting) urged the complete abolition of the death penalty. William Tallack (1831–1908), a London Friend, was secretary of the Society for the Abolition of Capital Punishment from 1863 to 1866, when he became secretary of the newly formed Howard Association for the Prevention of Crime, a post he filled for 35 years. Tallack was concerned not only to improve prison conditions but, similarly to Bellers' earlier insights, to tackle poor housing and unemployment, which he saw as the roots of much crime.

Indeed, treatment of prisoners and penal reform have been a longstanding and consistent concern of Quakers in many countries. Although the prison work of Elizabeth Fry (1780–1845) may have been more welfare oriented than rights based, at its core was the same understanding that despite being prisoners they should be treated as human beings. Fry may be the best known, but there were many other Quakers involved in assistance to prisoners and in penal reform from the early days of Quakerism. For example, William Tuke who in 1792 developed the concept of the asylum for the treatment of the mentally ill, thus removing them from prison,[4] and Geraldine Cadbury (1865–1941) who pioneered the creation of children's courts in the UK with a more relaxed atmosphere. Many Friends in other countries were also active in penal reform.

A more recent example

General issues about treatment of prisoners focused into the specific concern for the abolition of torture. Following consideration in 1974 by London Yearly Meeting, in 1976 the global Quaker body Friends World Committee for Consultation declared itself "to be utterly opposed to the use of torture and determined to spare no effort to bring it to an end", explaining that "We believe in the worth of every individual as a child of God, and that no circumstances whatsoever can justify practices intended to break bodies, minds and spirits."[5] Many Friends have remained active both in the specific Quaker Concern for the Abolition of Torture, and in other organisations such as Amnesty International (of which a Quaker, Eric Baker, was one of the initiators and subsequently secretary-general).

As is clear from this example, as well as from penal reform and concern for prisoners, these 'historic' examples have a continuity in today's Quaker concerns and work, both domestically and at the UN. Sometimes the same issues (or kinds of issues) persist, and sometimes they evolve, either because of changing understandings, or because one topic leads to another. In this context, it is interesting to see the way in which the historic work on the abolition of slavery evolved into the women's suffrage movement.

> In the progress of the anti-slavery movement experience revealed the great injustice, the detriment to human welfare, of the subordinate, disenfranchised condition of woman. Every step in that great reform was impeded by the inequality that depressed and degraded her. And these experiences were to the Abolitionists, in this, as in other directions, a liberal education. So, when the crime of slave-holding was overcome, they became the leaders in the women's suffrage cause … [6]

The same insights form the basis for Quaker human rights work today. Indeed there is continuity in many of the issues, with work either continuing on the same issues or evolving from the same root, as we shall see in the following examples of Quaker work on human rights at the UN.

CHAPTER 3

Why Quakers work at the UN

It is most important to use and develop the provisions of the charter for peaceful change of the status quo, so that fair and just conditions are created, which the nations are prepared to uphold.

(Konrad Braun, 1950)

That Quakers support the aims of the UN is not surprising. It was, after all, founded on ideals of peace, justice, respect for human rights and international law, and to promote social progress and better standards of life in larger freedom. In addition, it is dedicated to a principle in which Quakers believe, namely that truth is not a monopoly of the strong, rich or powerful.

The UN may be a flawed organisation which often does not live up to its ideals, but this can be seen as a reason to work with it and try to improve it, rather than one for abandoning it. The dilemma of supporting an organisation which is willing to use force (even as a last resort) had already arisen in relation to the League of Nations and continues with the UN. However, logically for Friends the distinction is not between supporting or rejecting the UN, but is about supporting its aims and some of its methods and activities without giving unconditional support to the organisation, while seeking to strengthen those aspects of which we approve and continuing to critique and challenge those we do not.

The roots of this kind of Quaker international engagement go back a long way. William Penn, in his *Essay towards the present and future peace of Europe* (1693), argued that

> if the Sovereign Princes of Europe would agree to meet by their stated deputies in a general Dyet, estate, or parliament, and there establish rules of justice for sovoraign princes to observe one to another; and thus to meet yearly, or in two or three years at farthest, or as they shall see cause; before which sovoraign assembly should be brought all differences between one sovoraign and another that cannot be made up by private embassies before the sessions begin: Europe would quietly obtain the so much desired and needed peace, to her harrassed inhabitants.[1]

In 1748, a Dutch Friend, Jan Van der Werf, acted as an emissary of Meeting for Sufferings in London, delivering a statement on the nature of a durable peace (as well as copies of Barclay's *Apology*) at the Aix-la-Chapelle meeting of plenipotentiaries.[2]

The idea of a permanent office (or Quaker embassy) came from

Carl Heath (1869–1950), who at a conference in Skipton, Yorkshire in 1917 pleaded for "the planting of a Quaker embassy in every European capital". The centres that were subsequently established, of which Geneva was one, were variable in duration and activities. These included visiting political and foreign prisoners,[3] minority issues,[4] refugees and statelessness, and through the Geneva Centre raising this issue with the Nansen office (predecessor of the UN High Commissioner for Refugees).[5] The Paris Centre undertook work on penal reform and the rights of conscientious objectors to military service,[6] and the Geneva Centre prepared a paper on "The rights of conscience and military service" and sent it to all the delegations to the 1933 Disarmament Conference.[7]

The establishment of the League of Nations in Geneva in 1920 attracted individual Quakers concerned for world peace, but 1926 was when the first official Quaker representatives (Bertram and Irene Pickard) were appointed to direct the Friends International Centre to express a Quaker view to the League and to inform Friends about the League and its activities. The Geneva Centre was re-established to work specifically at the UN once that organisation was created, and a Quaker Office to the UN in New York set up. In 1948, Friends World Committee for Consultation (which had been set up in 1937) was granted Consultative Status with the UN as an international non-governmental organisation (NGO) permitting it to attend, speak at, and submit written statements to many UN meetings. In 2002, it was accorded General Consultative Status, the highest category of NGO status, in recognition of the broad range of UN issues on which the QUNOs work.

Penn's idea is still very much the basis of Quaker work at the UN: the value of discussion and diplomacy rather than war and physical violence. In the same way, the Quaker UN work itself seeks to change perceptions and values through engagement and persuasion rather than trying to impose change by *force majeure*.

The Religious Society of Friends is a small body whose numbers count for little in the total of world forces assembled under UN auspices. Quakers have found their strength in the power of conviction which inspires their members, a conviction they seek constantly to renew and deepen as they face the world's need for peace and justice and the concept of a human family.[8]

Their work is not something remote from the rest of Friends' work overseas; it is not lobbying based on preconceived ideas or a one-track mind. Rather is it the opportunity to channel the experience of the Society in places where things can be changed.[9]

Working at the UN is not a substitute for local and national action, whether on human rights or the environment or peace.[10] The value of the UN is when there is a need for international or transnational solutions to problems. Or when external pressure on a government or other actors will assist in bringing about change, or preventing deterioration. For example, the UK only stopped routinely sending under-18s into combat because of the UN standards and pressure from other European countries to abide by them. Sometimes the UN can be a hindrance rather than a help because of its political dynamics, slow pace, or remoteness: powerful governments may seek to shelter those they consider allies or to use the system to pressurise their political opponents. However, even in these cases there are sometimes benefits – only Cuba was originally willing to challenge the USA directly by tabling a resolution on the "Question of arbitrary detentions in the area of the US naval base in Guantanamo" (L.88/Rev.2), in 2004. Their action forced a debate on the subject in the UN Commission on Human Rights even though they decided to withdraw the resolution given the likelihood of its being voted down.

QUNO seeks to both uphold and challenge the UN and the people who work in and around it – this includes understanding that this is an important institution but also a flawed one. So, it requires constructive engagement but also constructive criticism. At times, such an approach may look like excusing *realpolitik*, or having low expectations, or plain cynicism. However, I prefer to see it as realism, while maintaining our ideals and understandings about why, despite its flaws and frustrations, it is important. Certainly, Quaker work at the UN is not for everyone – if you want to see immediate and practical results 'on the ground', or seek the activity, solidarity and energy of activism (demonstrations, non-violent direct action, and so on), then the UN is not for you! But equally, the UN will not always be the most appropriate forum in which to seek the change desired, or may well be only one part of a broader strategy. In particular, it is important to keep recalling that the UN by itself cannot enforce change – even when it creates international law and this is accepted by the governments. It does not have enforcement powers, with the exception of that infamously flawed UN body, the Security Council; and the kind of enforcement powers it has are not always ones of which Quakers would approve.

CHAPTER 4

Why the particular human rights issues that QUNO takes up

I said to the man who stood at the gate of the year
"Give me a light that I may tread
safely into the unknown."
And he replied,
"Go into the darkness and put your
hand into the hand of God
That shall be to you better than light
and safer than a known way!"

(Minnie Louise Harkins, 1875–1957)

Issues and where they come from

Each issue that QUNO takes up has a different history and this will be illustrated by some examples, but it is important to remember two things, one substantive and one practical. First, not all issues, however important in themselves, will necessarily be appropriate to work at through the UN. The best line of action may be local or national or regional. Sometimes, there may be a specific channel within the UN system that can help without it becoming a major priority for QUNO. For example, Australian Quakers asked QUNO to assist when their government was reporting under the International Convention on the Elimination of All Forms of Racial Discrimination. The specific request was to support the two elderly indigenous elders from the Northern Territories who were coming to Geneva. QUNO's role was not long-lived or major in terms of the issues, but as a provider of advice about the UN human rights system and our best experiences of using it, as well as logistical support.

Second, in purely practical terms, QUNO is a small office. Most of the time in recent years the entire Human Rights and Refugees programme has consisted of two people, the Representative and one Programme Assistant (one-year junior professional position). In these circumstances, clearly it is possible to have a real impact only by having a limited number of priorities – in general I considered three was the absolute maximum at any one time. Having even that many priorities was only possible because the issues usually moved at different paces and rarely had 'crunch' points at the same time. In order to keep the workload and effectiveness levels remotely manageable, it is therefore important to define issues out as well as in. Thus although, for example, the abolition of torture is clearly a continuing Quaker concern, it is not in itself a current priority for QUNO because there are a number of effective NGOs working on it at the UN, and it is not clear what particular real benefit would be added by QUNO. (See below for QUNO's previous work on torture.) It is important to stress that this is not to suggest that Quaker involvement is not valuable, simply that QUNO involvement is unnecessary, while those Quakers who wish to be active could support and work through other NGOs. Indeed, I often joke about the number of "surrogate" Quaker NGOs there are, either because Quakers were involved in setting them up and/or because of the number of Quaker staff or members they have – and there is nothing wrong in that; indeed, it has a long history and has demonstrated considerable benefits, as with the establishment by Quakers and others of the Anti-Slavery Society in 1839 (see p. 9).

BOX 1: An example
In 2010, Australian Yearly Meeting Indigenous Concerns Committee asked QUNO for assistance to ensure that the Northern Territories Emergency Response (the Intervention) would be fully considered by the UN Committee on the Elimination of Racial Discrimination (CERD) to which the Australian government was reporting. 'Concerned Australians' funded Rosalie Kunoth-Monks from Central Australia and Djiniyini Gondarra from Arnhem Land in the North, who eagerly accepted, though not without some trepidation. Galiwin'ku on Elcho Island in Arnhem Land is a very long way from a post office from which you can lodge an application for a passport. The trip to Geneva started several weeks before arrival! QUNO took care of the Geneva end including arranging accommodation and transport, accreditation for the Committee meetings, organising other meetings, and explaining the UN processes and procedures, and what to expect. What we could not be certain was how CERD would react, but we need not have worried. The patent integrity and depth of feeling that Rosalie and Djiniyini brought, and the careful and detailed presentations they made, impressed CERD. The impact can be seen in the quality of the Concluding Observations that CERD adopted at the end of their consideration of the Australian report. Of course, CERD does not have enforcement powers, so this process will not in itself change Australian government policy, but it may be one factor in helping to do so. In any case, euphoria accompanied Rosalie and Djiniyini back to Melbourne. It was as though a great weight had been lifted from their shoulders. As Djiniyini stated, "We were able to present evidence first

hand. We were able to close the information gap." He continued, "We were able to speak from the soul. The environment in which we were speaking was one focused solely on human rights; it was not intruded upon by politics. We were able to reach the heights in dialogue and understanding that we hadn't expected."[1]

Quaker concerns

1. Child soldiers:[2] Dorothea Woods
(see the timeline in Box 2, p. 55)

The UN declared 1979 to be the International Year of the Child. In January 1979, Dorothea Woods wrote to the Clerk of Geneva (Switzerland) Monthly Meeting asking that the question of "Children Bearing Military Arms" be put on the Monthly Meeting agenda. Dorothea had become aware of child involvement in combat through two books. The first was Nicolas Hulot's *Ces Enfants qui souffrent*,[3] which showed children dying from malnutrition, disease and injury caused by wars and natural disasters, but also children fighting and being trained to fight in a number of countries in different parts of the world. Shortly afterwards Dorothea discovered a second book, Peter Townsend's *The smallest pawns in the game*,[4] which, in her own words, strengthened Hulot's 'cry of conscience'.[5] Writing in 1980, Dorothea herself described what happened:

> When considering what concern might best be linked with the International Year of the Child [1979], the Geneva Monthly Meeting thought that the historic Peace Testimony of Quakers gave them a responsibility to try to do something about the children bearing arms in civil wars, in wars for independence, and even in the international wars of our time....Our concern for these children came before the Quarterly Meeting of French-speaking Switzerland and then before the Yearly Meeting.

In June 1979 Switzerland Yearly Meeting minuted:

In this International Year of the Child, we wish to go on record against the practice of training children to kill and maim other human beings. We regret that the United Nations Declaration on the Rights of the Child [adopted in 1959] offers no protection even against the use of children in open fighting. We encourage the United Nations and the international organisations to press for measures against the participation of children in military training and action.

The Clerk of Geneva Monthly Meeting spoke to this concern at the Triennial Meeting of the Friends World Committee for Consultation (FWCC) in August 1979. It minuted:

Edna P. Legg has brought before us the concern of the Switzerland Yearly Meeting that Friends should register their abhorrence of the widespread involvement of children in military training and even in active combat. We unite with this concern and ask Yearly Meetings to take whatever action may be appropriate or necessary in their own countries to eliminate the militarisation of children.

This concern has been brought before us during the International Year of the Child which was proclaimed by the United Nations. We believe that the United Nations is the proper forum for the adoption of agreed measures against the participation of children in military training and action, and ask our Quaker United Nations Offices to pursue this concern.

Thus the Triennial not only endorsed the concern itself but also put a clear request to the Quaker UN Offices to work on the issue. In this context, it is important to recall that this was not simply a request from any Quaker body: QUNO represents FWCC at the UN. As the most broadly representative Quaker decision-making body and the sponsor of Quaker UN work, it has some authority to lay work on QUNO.

This is an example of the origin of an individual concern and its processing through the orthodox Quaker structures to become a corporate Quaker concern, while not relieving Dorothea herself of her determination to continue to work on the issue, which she did, writing to QUNO shortly before her death (in 2001) to express her appreciation for the progress that had been made at the UN. The issue came to be called 'child soldiers' and QUNO Geneva worked on it consistently for the following thirty years.

2. Women in prison: *Susan Hartshorne*

As already indicated, penal reform, and the treatment of prisoners – specifically of women prisoners – have been long-standing concerns of Quakers. The experience of imprisonment, both in the early days of Quakerism and more recently as conscientious objectors and for other acts of civil disobedience, has ensured a grounded realism for action.[6] A recent manifestation of this concern was the recognition by Susan Hartshorne, a British Quaker magistrate (Justice of the Peace), of the increasing number of women being sent to prison since at least 1998. As Susan describes it,

> I knew that the vast majority of the young people I saw in the Juvenile Courts came from dysfunctional families – very often with no fathers present. The young people had often been in care, their parents had often been in prison, and they rarely managed more than very basic literacy. I thought it obvious that the more women we put into prison, the more children we should see in our courts. If men go to prison they can rely on their women to look after the children. The reverse does not happen – if a mother is sent to prison the children suffer. They are sometimes taken into care or alternatively 'farmed out' with neighbours or relatives who often don't particularly want them. I tried hard to get our community facilities in this country better used – but we were then still being told that "prison works". Some of the community facilities I visited in the 1990s have, alas, since been closed.[7]

Having done some investigations of her own, Susan took the matter first to the Quakers in Criminal Justice (informal) group, and then in 2000 to the formal Quaker Peace & Social Witness (QPSW)

Crime and Criminal Justice Group.[8]

Although the Quaker UN Offices in Geneva and New York are the best known Quaker engagement with the UN, there is another long-standing strand of Quaker UN work: that on prison and criminal justice issues through the specialised UN processes relating to these areas. FWCC representatives have attended most of the five-yearly UN Crime Congresses and, in more recent years, the annual sessions in Vienna of the UN Commission on Crime Prevention and Criminal Justice. Thus it was natural that Susan's concern should be taken up initially through this FWCC representation to the UN's criminal justice bodies. However, women's imprisonment could equally be seen as a human rights issue and this led QUNO to also pursue it through the UN human rights bodies in Geneva. The FWCC Triennial in 2004[9] encouraged QUNO to continue. This led to joint work between the Vienna and Geneva Quaker UN representations[10] and, on 21 December 2010, to the UN adopting new specific UN Rules for the Treatment of Women Prisoners and Non-Custodial Measures for Women Offenders (Bangkok Rules) which had been negotiated through the UN Vienna process but with the primary Quaker involvement being QUNO.

3. Children of prisoners: a concern by evolution?

Often working on one issue leads to insights about other aspects of that issue or to other issues. An early example is the way the work on the abolition of slavery led to the campaign for the emancipation of women (see p. 11). In the current instance, it was a Ugandan Quaker, Stephen Guloba, who pointed to the children who were in prisons with their mothers and suggested that QUNO also needed to consider these. Having initially done so from the perspective of the women, what we learned, combined with the child-rights understanding developed during QUNO's work on child soldiers, led us to reverse the perspective and take a child-rights approach.

When looking at the situation through the child's eyes, many issues appear differently. For example, it may seem natural that the prison authorities should consider that allowing visitors to a prisoner is a privilege that can be withheld in the face of disciplinary infractions. However, the Convention on the Rights of the Child is clear that the child has a right to family contact (unless it is not in the child's best interests). Thinking about the children themselves led QUNO to the recognition that many more children of prisoners are not in prison with their parents, but are significantly affected by that imprisonment. It was interesting to discover when researching this book that these children were, indeed, part of Susan Hartshorne's original concern.

4. Death penalty

By at least 1818 London Yearly Meeting was united in calling for the abolition of capital punishment,[11] although John Bellers (see p. 10) and others had called for this, or at least its limitation, much earlier. QUNO made statements to the UN and worked in support of an Optional Protocol on abolition of the death penalty to the International Covenant on Civil and Political Rights between 1984[12] and 1989 when this protocol was adopted.

5. Conscientious objection to military service[13]

Rooted in the Peace Testimony, Quakers have corporately maintained their pacifist stance throughout the centuries and many individual Quakers have paid dearly for their conscientious objection to military service. In 1916, London Yearly Meeting insisted that, contrary to earlier practice, no exemption from conscription should be given for Quakers that was not equally applicable to other conscientious objectors[14] and acted to support all conscientious objectors.[15] The first FWCC statement on conscientious objection was submitted to the UN Commission on Human Rights in 1950[16] and may, indeed, have been the first FWCC statement to have been made to the UN.[17] Originally there was some hesitation over whether it was appropriate to use FWCC consultative status at the UN to pursue something which might be seen as narrow self-interest,[18] but, in line with the stance of London Yearly Meeting, QUNO worked on the issue on behalf of all conscientious objectors over succeeding years, mostly with little or no evidence of progress until 56 years later in 2006, when conscientious objection to military service was finally unequivocally recognised as being legally protected under the International Covenant on Civil and Political Rights. QUNO continues to follow up on this today, both strengthening the UN standards and helping local organisations to get it applied in practice.

6. *Torture*

As noted above, the use of torture has been a Quaker concern since 1974. The issue of torture was part of a Mohonk Conference organised by QUNO New York in 1977, and QUNO Geneva was involved in the drafting of the UN Convention against Torture (adopted in 1984). For several years,[19] FWCC contributed to the UN Voluntary Fund for the Victims of Torture (established in 1981) as an expression of Quaker witness, and QUNO was asked to chair the first meeting of contributors to that Fund.

QUNO has always been mindful of this Quaker concern and, where there were opportunities and benefits to being engaged, has not hesitated, while not maintaining the issue as a specific separate priority. For example, at the UN Commission on Human Rights in March 2002, the first one following the 9/11 attacks, and in the light of the challenge to the prohibition on torture, as well as other issues, QUNO was a strong and active supporter, with other major human rights NGOs, of the creation of a new mandate of Special Rapporteur on the Promotion and Protection of Human Rights while Countering Terrorism. Not only was QUNO able to bring its moral weight to the campaign, but also its good contacts with many governments which at that time the other human rights NGOs did not have. Equally, because of those contacts and good relationships, QUNO was able to engage and explain the fallacies of some of the proposals and arguments being put forward, as a result of which one ambassador stated that his government's position had changed (although this was not put to the test since the draft resolution had to be withdrawn in the face of concerted opposition). Strong opposition from the USA and opposition, or at least ambivalence combined with unwillingness to challenge the USA, by others led to that withdrawal, but the mandate was established in 2005. Indeed, Quaker House off-the-record discussions probably had a significant impact on the UN General Assembly's adoption without a vote of a resolution on Human Rights and Counter-Terrorism (following the initial unsuccessful attempt at the Commission).

7. *Refugees*

Part of the remit of the Friends International Centre in Geneva in the days of the League of Nations and subsequently, was to support the work of the High Commissioner for Refugees, in relation to refugees, and to displaced and stateless persons. This has remained part of QUNO's work throughout the years, although the specific focus changes: for example, sometimes more on women refugees, sometimes on children, sometimes on those in refugee-like situations within their own country. QUNO also has worked on the refugee/ asylum aspect of some other priority issues, such as child soldiers and conscientious objectors to military service (see pp. 23 and 27). Equally, with the tendency of governments to restrict access to asylum, many Quaker House lunches (see also p. 37) have sought to support those trying to maintain the focus and standards on refugee protection – governments, non-governmental organisations and UN staff – and to quietly challenge the negative attitudes towards those who seek to cross borders in search of asylum.

8. *Indigenous peoples*

The original Quaker insight of God in each individual, and the resulting obligations based on our common humanity, led in 1683 to the Treaty of Shackamaxon, between William Penn and the First Nations of the territory granted to him by Charles II.[20]

   The Quaker UN work on the rights of indigenous peoples was largely pursued by Canadian, American and Australian Friends, and in 2000 the Canadian Friends Service Committee (CFSC) was mandated by FWCC[21] to lead this work on behalf of Friends worldwide, facilitated and supported by the QUNOs. The formal beginnings of CFSC Quaker Aboriginal Affairs Committee were prefaced by a minute recorded by Canadian Yearly Meeting 1974:

> a confrontation between the Ojibway people of the [Kenora] area and various levels of government … has occupied our hearts and minds. We are concerned that active violence not erupt; and equally concerned that long standing grievances be understood, and all measures of settlement of those grievances be encouraged …

The benefits of this 'lead organisation' approach have included that QUNO has not needed to develop or recruit someone with expertise in the issues, but can facilitate the work by advising CFSC on UN processes, providing access to UN meetings and to government representatives and UN staff, hosting Quaker House events, and assisting with written and oral statements as necessary. At the same time, it has enabled the Quaker concern for the rights of indigenous peoples to be pursued at the UN, and has also given QUNO access to (and credit with) indigenous peoples' representatives which would not have occurred but for the expertise and standing of the Canadian Quaker representation. A key aspect of the work on this issue has been to support the positions of indigenous peoples and facilitate their representatives to speak for themselves by, for example, providing access to government delegations through hosting informal, off-the-record meetings at Quaker House at their request.

Individual and corporate witness

The examples given above all combine individual and corporate witness. Some represent an individual concern which was endorsed through Quaker channels, without absolving the individual from continuing to work on it. In the case of conscientious objection, this was a long-standing Quaker concern for which individual Quakers in many countries have suffered and worked to achieve national recognition. In the QUNO context, this may mean that several generations of QUNO staff work on an issue or that at a certain point QUNO's part is done, or mostly so, which does not absolve other Quakers from the need to continue work in their own contexts. For example, for better or worse, QUNO 'achieved' the Optional Protocol on Children in Armed Conflict, but the UK still recruits 16-year-olds. Addressing this has to be primarily a task undertaken within the UK, not at the UN, though UN processes may help to keep the pressure on the UK.

Power of initiative and identification of opportunities

Although QUNO's work comes from and through its 'parent bodies', it can also arise from the opportunities and ongoing development of concerns perceived by QUNO staff, subject always to testing through QUNO's committee process. Such testing is important to ensure that it is not merely a personal interest of an individual staff member or a transient issue, as well as to check that this should be Quaker UN work, and that QUNO time and resources should be used for it, given the small number of priorities which it is possible for QUNO to undertake at any one time and the long-term nature of much of the work and commitment. At the same time, QUNO staff may be best placed to see openings at the UN or linkages between issues, and too rigid a structure and process may inhibit the serendipitous opportunism that can be truly creative and productive.

A short-term example

During the expulsion of ethnic Albanians from Kosovo one of the concerns was the destruction of their identity and other documents. Once the NATO military ('humanitarian') intervention had started, Quakers and others who had sought alternative methods of dealing with the situation were feeling powerless and so met to discuss what our contribution could be, and in particular to focus on what would happen once the bombing stopped – realising that although we did not know when and under what circumstances, the bombing would stop at some point. The meeting was in Friends House, London, and was organised with Quaker assistance but under the name of one of the conflict transformation/resolution groups. I attended that meeting and in the course of it became aware that there were some issues which really needed to be considered by those developing the terms for ending the bombing and preparing the international presence. One of these related to the issue of documentation. Specifically, there was someone at the meeting who had worked for Friends in Bosnia and who talked about the problems which destruction of documentation creates – much more than an outsider like me would ever have realised as it is not just your passport or ID, but can affect your employment, health, property, tax and pension records and so on. Given his knowledge of both the issue and the region, I questioned him about all this and asked for his proposed solution. He pointed out that there must be a Central Records

Office and, therefore, the international community should demand that it be sealed in order to preserve the central records (from which individual IDs and documents could then be traced and replaced).

As soon as I returned to Geneva I contacted the representatives of some of the key governments, with all of whom I had extremely good relations at that time – the EU Presidency, the OSCE Chair-in-Office and a couple of others – asking whether they would be interested if I wrote them a briefing paper about this and some other issues. They all said yes, so I did that. As happens not infrequently in my work, I heard nothing further from any of them, not even an acknowledgement. Several months passed, the bombing had stopped, and Sergio Vieira de Mello was appointed by the UN to take care of Kosovo. I was at a small party of human rights and humanitarian people during which we were arguing vociferously about Kosovo, the military action, the role of NGOs and so on, when one person commented that when Sergio arrived in Kosovo he did a remarkable thing: he immediately ordered the sealing of the Central Record Office in Pristina. Of course, we cannot prove cause and effect … although one of the diplomats with whom I had communicated repeatedly stated his admiration for the Quakers' 'lateral thinking' at his farewell reception.

A longer-term example

Starting in 2003, QUNO's work was originally focused very much on imprisoned women themselves. It was through the FWCC Triennial that a Ugandan Friend highlighted the need to also look at children imprisoned with their mothers. QUNO duly took up this issue, initially considering the situation from the perspective of the mother, and only subsequently drawing on the experience of the earlier work on child soldiers, bringing a child-rights perspective to bear. Later again, QUNO's focus broadened to encompass the larger group of children with imprisoned parents (mother, father or both) and who are not in prison with the parent, as well as the children who are. Similarly, QUNO's exposure to the rights of indigenous peoples ensured that the situation of indigenous women prisoners would be brought in, and the work on refugees and statelessness brought the recognition of the problems which can occur when a foreign national prisoner gives birth and the baby cannot stay in the prison with the mother or reaches the age for removal from prison. At the time of this 'evolution' (see pp. 26–7), QUNO was not aware that Susan Hartshorne's original concern had encompassed children of prisoners as well as women in prison, but perhaps this illustrates the way in which a concern can be generated in more than one individual. Many of the examples given above undoubtedly had a number of progenitors even if we tend to associate them with one individual because this is the record that has come down to us or because one became best known or most associated with the particular issue.

A QUNO-identified concern?

QUNO's expertise in the UN system and strategic thinking is often sought by those wishing to bring forward new issues or make better progress on those already raised. In the case of Internally Displaced Persons[22] (IDPs) – those in a refugee-like situation but who have not crossed an internationally recognised border – QUNO hosted a key meeting at Quaker House in February 1990 at which Roberta Cohen (Refugee Policy Group) presented the issue to about thirty governments and others. As well as hosting strategy meetings, QUNO did much of the lobbying at the UN Commission on Human Rights together with the World Council of Churches and, subsequently, Caritas Internationalis, while the Refugee Policy Group provided the substance. In due course, this led to the creation of the position of Representative of the UN Secretary General on IDPs and the development of the Guiding Principles on Internal Displacement.

QUNO's work on different issues often leads to it gaining expertise which it did not originally have and consequent creative and insightful understandings of linkages which tend to get overlooked, sometimes of a quite technical nature. For example, earlier QUNO work on women refugees combined with ongoing discussions about the high proportion of women amongst refugee and displaced populations, and the ideal of returning home, led QUNO to identify the flaw in the argument in countries where women cannot own land or property and to undertake a short focused piece of work on that issue.[23]

Conclusion

What have been highlighted here are some of the major, long-term priority areas of work. QUNO frequently picks up – using its power of initiative within the parameters of the agreed work priorities – smaller, short-term pieces. Some of these are in the form of support or assistance to parts of our Quaker constituency (see, for example, the Australian report to the UN Committee on the Elimination of Racial Discrimination given in Box 1, p. 22). Others are on more technical aspects of UN work – for example, assisting the UNHCR campaign for the ratification of the two conventions relating to statelessness, or supporting their and other NGOs' efforts to increase birth registration amongst refugee and displaced populations (as well as more generally). Although Quakers have not *per se* pronounced on these issues, they are fundamental to the general Quaker insight of the value of each individual, and they also come up in relation to other aspects of the priority areas of work. For example, one form of discrimination against women is their inability to transmit nationality to their children in some countries, and this can create problems for the babies born to foreign national women prisoners.

CHAPTER 5

How Quakers work at the UN

In times of difficulty remind yourself of the value of prayer, of perseverance and of a sense of humour.

(Advices & queries, 23)

There are many commonalities in how Quakers work at the UN whoever the individual staff member and whichever office is involved. These include common methods such as the traditional Quaker House informal, off-the-record lunches, as well as common principles which may be practised in different ways, such as the models of engagement with the UN. Some of the differences arise because of the different possibilities which the UN presents in relation to areas of work. For example, the UN human rights bodies are much more accessible to direct input from NGOs than are its disarmament ones or the World Trade Organisation.[1]

Sometimes it is the issue, and how to advance it most effectively, which dictates different approaches, even by the same staff member. For example, recruitment into the armed forces is a central government function, whereas the management of prisons is often a regional or local government one. Some issues, such as children of prisoners, are little known and so require research to understand them and change perceptions, while others, such as conscientious objection to military service, are more susceptible to a legal approach. Of course, these are all generalisations, and often the real nature of conscientious objection is as little understood as the impact on children of having a parent in prison.

At the same time, because so much Quaker UN work is bound up with the person undertaking it at any one time, each individual will bring to it their own particular skills, approaches and ideas. Since one of the characteristics of Quaker UN work is the relatively long duration of staff, another feature is learning from experience – both in the sense of what worked well or did not work well on a particular issue, and in analysing the similarities and differences between the issues on which we work and, therefore, what we might want to try on this particular occasion and why.

Quaker House lunches

I pin my hopes to quiet processes and small circles in which vital and transforming events take place. (Rufus Jones)

One of the hallmarks of QUNO work is the 'Quaker House lunch'.

Many of these do actually include lunch, although some may be over dinner, or coffee and biscuits. However, lunchtime around the UN presents particular opportunities because there is a two-hour break between the normal scheduled UN meeting times of 10am–1pm and 3pm–6pm. This is long enough for people to get together and have a real discussion, but equally, and if lunch is provided, is a confined time so that the participants know the 'limits' of their commitment. This may mean that there is a need for a series of such lunches in order to cover more ground, or for a half-day, full-day or longer conference from time to time. There is also a Quaker tradition of such longer meetings.

One of the points, therefore, is sheer availability. Most people are likely to be available unless they have particular commitments, while many people prefer to go home or to go out in the evening, and breakfast meetings conflict with preparation for the day's UN meetings and dealing with other work requirements.

Each Quaker representative tends to do Quaker House lunches differently – just as each has a personal approach to the substance of the work. In part, this reflects the different personalities and approaches; in part the different issues and ethos of those working on them. Some are more inclined to dinners or conferences, to expert speakers and external 'chairs', to more or less elaborate food.

What is it that makes these events special and different from meetings and lunches organised by others? I can only provide my own reflections and analysis, taking into account comments from the participants.

Shortly after I arrived in 1993, I decided to try starting a series of Quaker House lunches in response to my own analysis and perception at that time that in the human rights field there was virtually no discussion going on across the five UN regional groups[2] and that some of the problems which arose in relation to human rights issues at the then UN Commission on Human Rights[3] were because of this. I was convinced that some problems could be solved if there was better and more genuine communication. One diplomat described to me the 'consultations' which took place as being one group coming and 'telling' the other on what they wanted their support. I heard for myself diplomats from one group saying that they did not understand why 'they' (others) did not support 'our' initiatives – and yes, using 'them' and 'us' designations. Translating it into UK parliamentary terminology, what I perceived was that these diplomats, while making no effort to reach out, expected government representatives from other regions to 'cross the floor of the House' to vote with them.

I was in a position to identify these trends and feelings not only because I monitored the work of the Commission but also because of building contacts with diplomats from different countries and regions. At that time, this was unusual in that the tendency of human rights NGOs was to work predominantly with 'Western' governments – one of the differences for QUNO was that the child soldier issue brought us into conflict with the interests of a number of Western governments but more positive engagement with many from other regions. In addition, QUNO's perceived objectivity in our reporting on the Commission on Human Rights – not politically aligned to Western group positions – and the fact that we did not make public denunciations about human rights violations in named countries, but instead worked thematically on human rights issues, all contributed to the perception that QUNO was 'different' from other human rights NGOs.

One of the important aspects – and privileges – of working for QUNO is the opportunity to experiment, to try things which may not work. This was very much the spirit of this venture. The idea was to try to see whether it was possible to build a group of diplomats from different regions where issues could be discussed – very informally, all off-the-record. My thinking was that such discussions would avoid some problems, although I did not imagine that they would solve all the problems because there are, indeed, some profound and real differences. But, again, if people understood why they had such differences we could, as I put it, 'disagree better'. So, there was no specific 'measurable' objective; no attempt to force a 'result' or a consensus, but an opportunity to explore and discuss and get to know people from other countries and regions. But, how to get people to come and, if they came, how to get them to talk…?

Before starting, I gave a lot of thought to the group dynamics. What was likely to make people feel more relaxed; what kind of topic

– not too threatening but something that everyone had an interest in and could contribute to a discussion about; what kind of food; the physical arrangements including the Arthurian Round Table approach with no head or foot and with seating that enabled all to see each other easily. The formula I came up with was that the group should be small enough so that everyone could sit round one table and participate in the discussion. Since there are five UN regional groups, by inviting two from each group, no-one would be "isolated" but the gathering would be a good size for a proper discussion. Initially, I did not include any other NGOs – reaching the stage that some of these could be included was a major step forward and is now standard practice. There was enough initial tentative interest to make it worth trying – and for that first meeting I did not suggest that this might be the start of a process, merely an invitation to one discussion on this particular topic.

As things developed, I have been able to increase the size and change the composition of the group – both including more or fewer delegates from one or other region, and bringing in other NGOs. However, whenever I am seeking to start a new group or begin on a new issue, I go back to basics in thinking through the principles again, even if this does not lead to precisely the same format.

One thing which strikes me as a Quaker is the degree of formality and status consciousness at the UN and within the diplomatic community. This is one of the major differences between the meetings we organise and others.

Food is remarkably important: it can be a help or a hindrance. Apart from all the obvious religious and cultural issues, there are also personal ones – at one time, my regular group included someone with a gluten allergy and another with a lactose problem. I try to remember these points for those who come regularly, and continually encourage the participants to tell me about their needs and likes. Food that is enjoyable so that people look forward to coming, but is not the object of the exercise, is the balance we seek. We have clearly been successful in that there are regular jokes about suffering withdrawal symptoms because we are not organising enough lunches with the now famous ratatouille quiche from our local bakery (and occasional suggestions for fundraising by producing and selling a

Quaker House cookbook).

More seriously, there is the question of what kind of food is detrimental to discussion – for example, trying to bone a fish tends to detract from concentrating on and participating in a discussion. We also tend to informal, buffet-style self-service, which not only increases informality but enables people to decide how much of what they would like. There is a real sense of achievement when a participant feels at home enough to start with dessert rather than the main course – not something I have observed at any other lunch meetings! Again, having free seating rather than set places means that the participants can choose where, and next to whom, they wish to sit – though if required, I am prepared to split up cliques! The other side of this is trying to ensure that no one is or feels isolated – physically, geographically, substantively, or because they are new to the group. Mostly, of course, this is what you would expect from any host.

Even apart from the practicalities of the food and arrangements, is the sense of tapping into long traditions of the creation of trust and community by sitting round and sharing food together – an insightful comment from a participant who also happened to be an anthropologist. Again it is worth stressing that the commonest other lunch-time events are either formal diplomatic events, or grabbing a sandwich to eat hastily before the discussion begins. Whatever the disadvantages of eating and talking at the same time, the sense of community created by 'breaking bread' and sitting together, is worth the inconvenience.

Another important point is not ambushing people: I include not only the topic of discussion but also the list of invitees in the invitation so others know who else to expect. Equally, by starting with a round of introductions means that everyone knows who is there and can identify each other. The routine introduction also reminds participants of the Quaker House ground rules – that everything is informal, including both the self-service nature of the food and the discussion which is also off-the-record, and explanations of what the food is, what the procedure is, and so on so that everyone knows and feels comfortable about it. Having previous participants always helps to set the tone. The feel of Quaker House itself: the fact that it is a house, not a conference room, restaurant or office block, but actually feels like a family home, and that people can wander out into the garden before or after the meeting weather permitting. One participant, arriving for the second time, automatically took off his jacket and tie, and then hastily checked that this was all right, commenting that it felt like the home of his Lutheran pastor grandfather.

QUNO being an NGO means that Quaker House is indeed neutral territory between the government representatives, as well as being clearly informal. The fact that we choose who to invite means that we do not have to be politically correct and invite, say, the EU Presidency or a regional group coordinator, where a government might feel obliged to, even if they were not the most useful person to have present. If others learn of discussions that they think they should have been invited to (and inevitably they often do), it is 'only QUNO' who is to blame, including where necessary being prepared to refuse to invite people who seek an invitation. Having clear objective criteria for this really helps!

Expectation predicates behaviour: as the reputation of Quaker House lunches and the expectation that people *will* behave differently is created, participants tend to conform to those expectations. So success breeds success. Some regular participants clearly develop their own strategies too: floating ideas to see what the reaction is or what might happen if they changed their position somewhat, in a context where it is no loss of face to go back or to decide not to pursue the idea; making an apparently indiscreet comment or revelation that encourages others to 'open up', and taking on the role of comic relief or naive questioner. These latter roles more often fall to QUNO, in order to break the ice or defuse a tense situation.

In the early days, it would have been impossible to have brought in, say, Amnesty International or Human Rights Watch, because some of the diplomats were from countries subject to severe public criticism by those NGOs and would have been unlikely to come. Over a period of years, and as diplomats gained confidence in the process, it became possible slowly to bring in other NGOs who also understood the nature and purpose of these lunches. Not all NGO representatives proved able or willing to differentiate this process from other interactions between NGOs and other governments, and to accept the fact that it is possible to discuss a topic with representatives of a government that is committing human rights violations. This led, on one occasion, to a diplomat commenting, "We don't talk to each other like that *here!*"

Successes, yes, but also failures. The process does not always work. One of the limitations is that the participants need to be people who are individually able and willing to engage in this kind of discussion – some people talk too much and will not let others talk, or simply contradict them. Some are not willing to say anything, though happy to listen. Clearly some of these gained a lot from the discussion and would happily discuss with me at length afterwards, but their silent presence disturbed the sense of a fully engaged discussion by all the participants. Others continue to state and re-state their government or group's position. Sometimes it is the linguistic limitations of the organiser which makes it hard to reach out, though we have held bilingual discussions from time to time, with all deemed to at least understand both French and English, but free to speak the one they preferred.

Do some governments seek to exploit us? Undoubtedly. Sometimes this is not a problem as their aim is at least consonant with (if not the same as) ours. Sometimes this is not the case, or it is not just one government, but the discussion moves in directions that are not in accord with Quaker objectives. At times, I have found it necessary to intervene in the discussion, either quite explicitly expressing disquiet or to steer it in another direction.

Sometimes it is a question of negotiating with the main proponent of an issue that they will not attend the discussion, in order to allow a freer and franker exchange of views. Occasionally flatly refusing a request for an invitation when a government or NGO has heard about a lunch and seek to invite themselves! An example was not inviting Australia to some of our discussions on refugee protection at a time when it was not only treating asylum seekers badly domestically but was seeking to promote its approach at the UN, and part of our objective was to counter this. By contrast, sometimes it is precisely a government that is behaving badly that needs to be brought into the discussions, in particular if one of their neighbours or someone 'like-minded' is there, who is actually addressing the same or similar problems in a much better way, and who can share this experience and the rationale for it with them.

Some of the successes were unexpected. For example, QUNO's early cross-regional human rights discussions were credited by the participants for enabling the first consensus resolution on the Right to Development, though this was not a specific intention and QUNO was not involved in that issue. The links and confidence engendered amongst those participating in the discussions were seen as a crucial factor in the outcome.

Some successes were hoped for, though not necessarily 'expected' – the one cited frequently by other human rights NGOs was the discussion between some members of the African group and a small number of NGOs about the proposed Code of Conduct for Special Procedures (see p. 68, and Glossary pp. 92–3). This enabled the underlying concerns from both 'sides' to be explored and discussed, developing better understanding of all parties involved, with resulting changes to the text. As one participant commented, it was the first time that anyone had actually talked with them about the substance of the issues. The snag was that this lunch discussion became so widely known that it created a backlash against some of the participants because others had not wished an 'improved' result. QUNO therefore had to work hard and proactively to 're-establish' the non-threatening nature of Quaker House lunches in order to enable participants to be able to come without allegations of 'treason' from other members of their regional group.

One of the factors which has been beneficial for QUNO in developing our diplomatic contacts is working on refugee issues as well as on human rights. Logically and conceptually, this could be a human rights programme and it could then encompass human rights of refugees and displaced persons. But because of the UN structure whereby refugees are generally considered to equate with UNHCR and humanitarian issues, while human rights is "only" those institutions and bodies which say 'human rights' in the name, it helps to spell out that the programme has this double focus. With the government Missions (delegations) to the UN, the larger ones also make a distinction between their staff who work on human rights and those who work on humanitarian issues. However, smaller delegations do not have the luxury of the resources to make that distinction, and indeed, some individuals are also covering the World Health Organisation (WHO) and other UN agencies as well. During some of the tense political confrontations on human rights issues, QUNO and other refugee NGOs were able to build good relations with some developing-country representatives because of the restrictive asylum and immigration policies by countries such as Australia and the EU. In particular, this enabled QUNO to build good links with a number of African delegations at a time when there was little contact and a lot of mistrust between human rights NGOs and African delegations.

Consonance of ends and means

The need to practise what we preach is not unique to Quaker UN work but should be inherent in all Quaker work. In this context it includes, for example, that if we want to encourage the use of dialogue, and real listening and engagement, then we also have to practise these in our work. Similarly, if the promotion and protection of human rights in general as well as specific rights is one of our aims, then we must respect the rights of those we are dealing with. One of the specific issues that has come up in this context is using photographs of identifiable people, for example of child soldiers or women prisoners, without their knowledge and consent. Another example is listening to and respecting the wishes of the NGOs or individuals we work with in the different countries so that, for example, in one country conscientious objectors to military service may want to have an alternative civilian service whereas in another they may also object to alternative service. Of course, we explain to the best of our ability the consequences (and limits of international law) in relation to their position, but the final decision has to be theirs, and QUNO's task is to provide the best legal arguments and access to UN procedures to try to achieve their aims (always of course within the parameters of our mutual overall objective).

Maintaining Quaker truthfulness in the context of politically charged negotiations and processes can be a challenge. As Tony Stoller put it in his Swarthmore Lecture:

It is clear that to achieve change in many of the areas which are of concern to us we need thorough research, a wide coalition of interests, access to the points of power and decision, and the ability to influence them. That means joining together in an approach which can enter the gates of policy-making to be heard there, as well as demonstrating a wide level of support outside the walls. That is not inconsistent with our principles. It only becomes so when we find ourselves asked to keep the company of groups who would act in a way we find unacceptable. In that circumstance we would not accept that any end can justify the means to be used. But short of such a position, we need to be open to the leadings of others, and the things they can bring to a collective enterprise …. The plain speaking of truth to power means having something well thought through to say, and then seeking the opportunity to say it to the right people to good effect.[4]

I would add two things. First, speaking truth to power is better done in a way that makes it more likely that 'power' will actually 'hear' what we have to say, rather than automatically resisting or dismissing it. Second, when articulating our objectives we may need to be clear what is our ultimate aim and what are intermediate steps in that direction. For example, opposition to all armed forces does not preclude working to prevent children being enrolled, nor does advancing the right of conscientious objection to military service require the acceptance of conscription. We may, therefore, need to be careful in our thinking, drafting and statements to ensure that, in these instances, we neither say nor imply that we accept the legitimacy of conscription as long as it is not children or conscientious objectors.

At the same time, it is important to recognise that we may have mutual interests in some areas while having radically different views in others. For example, on conscientious objection to military service, QUNO has worked with and for Jehovah's Witnesses, and indeed I have joked that the National Rifle Association of the USA, with their slogan "guns don't kill people; people kill people", might be a useful ally in convincing those Balkan governments who refuse conscientious objection status to anyone who has ever had a gun licence that someone might genuinely object to shooting people while being willing to shoot rabbits.

Sometimes we may have mutual interests with particular governments (or some parts of a government) or with members of the various UN secretariats, or human rights experts within the UN system, as well as with other NGOs. This needs to be seen in the context of our understanding that no-one has a monopoly of the truth and of being willing to talk to anyone, and, therefore, our assumption that at some times there will be many who will share or partially share our objectives. When this is the case we can work with them to advance our objectives, and when we disagree or our interests diverge, we go our separate ways.

Within the political system of the UN, ideas are often rejected because of their source rather than being considered on their merits: one of QUNO's contributions can be to look at the substance rather than the author – and sometimes espouse or at least articulate the ideas ourselves in order to help others to overcome their objection to the author.

In the human rights area, it is far from unusual for a state to have a vested interest in a particular issue. For example, it is no accident that the Russian Federation took up the issue of arbitrary deprivation of nationality following the dissolution of the Soviet Union, but this does not invalidate the fact that such deprivation is a serious human rights problem which deserves to be addressed. This was precisely one of the opportunities for QUNO to step in and work with the Russian delegation, and encourage other governments to engage on the substance of the proposed resolution in order to produce a good, general text.

Agenda-setting

One of the best aspects of Quaker work is that we have always tried to seek out areas where new initiatives are needed. We have taken those initiatives. We have opened the eyes of people around us. We have encouraged other organisations to take up the same type of work, ... And then, when enough people have got their eyes opened, we have stepped back and tried to focus our attention on other areas, not yet discovered by the general public.[5]

QUNO is not just reactive, responding to the UN agenda and requests, although we often do that too and seek creative ways to bring 'our' issues within the existing agenda; but it has actually put things onto the UN and international agenda, for example child soldiers, internally displaced persons (IDPs), women in prison and children of prisoners.

If we are true to our vision of identifying new issues, then it is almost inevitable that we will have to find ways to get them onto the agenda. This can sometimes be a long and frustrating process. Although QUNO was able to raise the issue of children of prisoners within existing UN agenda items and processes, it took several years – undertaking and publishing research, infiltrating the issue into other agendas by making links not apparent to others (for example, that imprisoning a parent is one of the ways in which the state deprives children of parental care), and so on – before it became sufficiently recognised and pressing for it to appear in UN documents and resolutions, and for the Committee on the Rights of the Child to decide (at the third time of asking) to devote a Day of General Discussion[6] to it in September 2011.

However, it is not only the UN agenda that needs to be influenced. QUNO – and Quakers – cannot achieve much alone. We need allies to reach our objectives: this was one of the keys to success of the campaign to abolish the slave trade (see p. 9). This may entail identifying others who are concerned about the issue, or persuading others that they should be! This is essential in order to achieve our objectives. Furthermore, it is usually the case that the nature of our issues is such that they are rarely completely resolved and so continued work is needed, though this may be of different sorts and at different levels. For example, once new UN standards are created, they still have to be implemented, and their implementation monitored. Because QUNO is such a small organisation, if we are not to work on the same issues in perpetuity, we also need to get others engaged in our issues in order to be able to move on, confident in the knowledge that our part is done and the work in that area will be continued by others.

One of the benefits of the UN human rights system is that it has monitoring procedures so that an issue that is integrated into their work will be regularly and routinely followed up with governments, thus continuing to draw attention to the issue and putting pressure on states to do something about it. At the same time, without a specific focus of energy or attention – and usually that means involvement of NGOs – there is an inherent danger of loss of interest or profile as new issues come along. So, for example, QUNO not only proactively sought the involvement of other NGOs in the work on child soldiers, but helped to set up the Coalition to Stop the Use of Child Soldiers,[7] and only ceased to have the issue as one of its priorities when we were confident that others would continue the work.

The media can be important allies in getting issues on the agenda, in developing the understanding and maintaining the interest in them. The work on child soldiers, for example, was significantly assisted by being taken up by a journalist at a relatively early stage, and subsequently as QUNO's research came out providing good opportunities for interviews to explain the issues and our findings.

Advocacy: Engagement and persuasion vs confrontation

One of the arguments I used to hear a lot was: "Quakers do peace; Amnesty International does human rights"; the implication being that Quakers should not be doing human rights work. There were two aspects to this. One was about human rights itself; the other about campaigning or lobbying.

Even within this framework some issues, such as child soldiers or conscientious objection to military service, could be justified as QUNO priorities because they were at the interface of peace/war and human rights. In fact, when I started working at QUNO in 1993 all the specific priority human rights issues on which QUNO was working could be articulated as being at the intersection of human rights and armed conflict – child soldiers, conscientious objection to military service, internally displaced persons. To these I added work on fundamental standards of humanity (human rights in armed conflict and internal strife).

There is a logic to Quakers working at this interface point, precisely because of Quaker views about war and peace, and, in particular, that those who oppose war should be supported, and that people, particularly children, should not be acculturated into it. Furthermore, at that time there were few if any other 'human rights NGOs' working at that intersection point, and so there was also a particular need and niche for Quaker work there. The more general 'gap' in human rights NGO coverage is no longer the case, and the child soldier issue has become mainstreamed into the work of many UN bodies and NGOs. However, there may still be particular Quaker insights to be applied in this area, for example, bringing restorative justice into the creation or rebuilding of criminal justice systems in post-conflict situations.

However, the limitation of the linkage between peace and human rights fails to do justice to both the Quaker conviction of the value of each individual human being (and the long history of engagement with human rights issues) and the recognition that conflicts may arise because of injustice and ill-treatment, and thus the need for peacemakers to find non-violent means of redressing these.[8] Indeed, it may be argued that the UN and regional human rights systems are one of the non-violent avenues available for action on such issues.

The second part of the "Quakers don't do human rights" idea was that Quakers should be reconcilers and neutral facilitators rather than advocates of a particular position whereas anything to do with human rights was confrontational and should, therefore, be avoided. This reflected the traditional dichotomy between 'prophets and reconcilers'.[9] The parallel tension between 'visionaries' and 'realists' has different dimensions: can one keep the absolutist vision while taking slow, partial, intermediate steps,[10] and can one act as a facilitator or bridge-builder as well as an advocate? For example, should Quakers refuse to support the work of the International Committee of the Red Cross and the development and implementation of the Geneva Conventions and their Additional Protocols because we are opposed to war and these 'only' seek to mitigate war's effects by regulating the conduct of warfare? Or, in the case of child soldiers, should

Quakers not have sought to eliminate the use of children in armed forces since we are opposed to armed forces *per se*? This argument was relayed to me by some Quakers who refused to participate in the efforts to stop this use of children.

Although the approach of some of the major international human rights NGOs has changed over the years, what might be termed the 'classic' human rights approach is the public denunciation through the media of particular policies and practices of named governments. Is this what *Quaker* human rights work at the UN is about or is it different from say that of Amnesty International or Human Rights Watch (to name two of the best known and most high profile and influential human rights NGOs)?

Because Quakers are a *religious community* with membership in different countries, one of the strengths and challenges for Quaker work on human rights is that it is not appropriate to publicly denounce human rights violations in specific countries, *unless the Quakers in that country wish it.*[11] However, it is not only for this reason that QUNO rarely uses this methodology. We are seeking more than 'behavioural compliance', that is following the rules because they are the rules. We seek transformation – the changing of perceptions and understandings. One of the challenges for QUNO is that if you believe that there is something of God in everyone, then this applies also to the government representatives. This has various consequences. 'Government' ceases to be perceived as a single monolithic inhuman entity – indeed, within any government there tend to be not only separate departments with different and often competing interests, but also individuals with divergent viewpoints, some more open or 'progressive' (that is aligned with our thinking) than others – though again this may vary depending on the specific issue. Indeed, it may be the personal experience of the individual which leads them to want not only to support 'our' initiative but also to change their own government's policy. On child soldiers one of our strongest and most consistent supporters had lost his younger brother in this way.

More generally, then, QUNO's role is to try to understand what brings about change, both generically and also in specific instances: how does this relate to this particular issue, in this country or group of countries, and at the UN. Part of working at the 'political level' – and this is not only true of the UN, of course – is identifying where the points of potential change are and how to use and reinforce them. This may be sympathetic individuals or departments within the system, or professionals and practitioners. One of the lessons from our work on women in prison was discovering how often it is the prison professionals themselves who are keenest to change and improve things; providing them with information, analysis, comparisons with and ideas from other countries or systems gives them tools that they can use both to make changes and to advocate for them.

In my own experience of Quaker UN work the questions about advocacy and facilitation form a creative tension – and I am aware that at times I may have got it wrong – which is less about not being able to do both, but about *how* one does advocacy. Duncan Wood describes how Quakers

> continue to believe in the power of the Spirit manifested in human lives. They do not believe that humanity is in the grip of vast, impersonal forces beyond its control; they do believe that our problems can and will be overcome by dedicated men and women. Generations of experience in acting on this have taught Friends to listen quietly and patiently, to speak frankly without giving offence, to be impartial, conscientious and discreet, thus winning the trust and confidence of others.[12]

If indeed, we have contact with and the confidence of our interlocutors, and use the right tone and approach, we may be able to 'advocate', to 'tell it as it is' and to suggest alternatives, without being confrontational. For example, having researched the question of child soldiers in Colombia, I repeatedly raised directly with government representatives the results of that research – in particular, the link between young people not being in school, and being physically and, in the case of girls also sexually, abused at home or in wider domestic settings, and their joining armed groups. Of course, it can be very helpful to have someone else at the same time keeping the pressure on by public denunciation of the government's human rights violations! Similarly, with clear information about the laws and actual situation in the countries concerned, I have constantly engaged with various governments about their policies and practices in relation to conscientious objectors, seeking not only to complain but also to explain the problems as well as the rationale behind conscientious objection.

Clearly, as we are an office to the UN, the various parts of that organisation are our main interlocutors, but in many different forms. We have used public UN human rights meetings in order to raise awareness of and educate governments, NGOs, UN secretariat staff and human rights experts in various UN capacities about 'our' issues. Secondly, we have used the UN to create new standards (such as the Optional Protocol on the Involvement of Children in Armed Conflict) or new interpretations of existing ones (such as the protection of conscientious objection under the right to freedom of thought, conscience and religion). Once established, these standards will continue to be used and applied by the UN in its relations with governments. Because of the expertise developed by QUNO, I have been commissioned by the UN to produce materials, for example, the child soldiers research[13] for the UN Study on the Impact of Armed Conflict on Children (Machel Report), a study for the International Labour Organisation (ILO) on why adolescents volunteer for armed forces and groups,[14] a draft *Handbook on conscientious objection to military service* for the Office of the UN High Commissioner for Human Rights, and a background paper and draft guidelines on conscientious objection to military service, draft evasion, desertion and asylum for the UN High Commissioner for Refugees (UNHCR).

However, at different times there have been parts of the UN system, or groups outside it, with whom QUNO has felt it important to engage in order to further our issues. The International Labour Organisation (ILO) involvement in child soldiers became possible with the research undertaken by QUNO for the Machel Study which, for the first time, identified the categories of children who are most likely to become child soldiers and the recognition that these were the same groups as the child labourers. The acceptance that child soldiering was in fact a specific form of child labour was a conceptual breakthrough in the understanding of the issue, as well as opening the door to the inclusion of child soldiering in the ILO's Convention No. 182 on the Worst Forms of Child Labour. Equally important on child soldiers was the role of the Red Cross (both the International Committee of the Red Cross and the national Red Cross and Red Crescent Societies). Thus QUNO was involved in several of the International Conferences of the Red Cross and Red Crescent Movement. At the same time, QUNO made a particular effort to engage the World Council of Churches on this issue (at their General Assembly in Zimbabwe). More recently (2009), the World Council of Churches background study (with which QUNO assisted informally) and Central Committee minute on conscientious objection to military service (a process possibly initiated by the Quaker on the Central Committee) to mark the end of its Decade to Overcome Violence, has been an asset in continuing and expanding the engagement with the WCC and its member churches. On women in prison QUNO has not only worked with the UN Office on Drugs and Crime and the UN Commission and Congress on crime prevention and criminal justice, but also with the Europe Office of the World Health Organisation, whose Health in Prisons Project approached us having become aware of the particular issues around health and women prisoners through QUNO's work.

At times, it may be beneficial to the objectives for QUNO not to take a public stand. For example, where there is a joint NGO statement on a particular issue, it may be advantageous to 'throw QUNO's weight' behind it, but equally, it may be better to not sign QUNO on publicly, in order to leave the freedom to engage different actors without already having taken a specific position on the issue. Sometimes this is purely a strategic question. Sometimes it is because other NGOs would like to be more strident or criticise specific governments. Of course, there may also be an actual divergence of views.

BOX 2: Timeline on child soldiers

1979: International Year of the Child. Child Soldier concern raised in Geneva Monthly Meeting and Switzerland Yearly Meeting and endorsed by FWCC Triennial. QUNOs asked to work on the issue. QUNO Geneva advocates inclusion of prohibition of child recruitment and use in military action in draft Convention on the Rights of the Child.

1989: Convention on the Rights of the Child adopted with provision on child recruitment and use in hostilities but only under 15 years of age.

1991: Council of Delegates of the International Red Cross and Red Crescent Movement adopts resolution No. 14 on child recruitment and use in hostilities proposed by Swedish and Icelandic Red Cross, and in 1995 endorses a Plan of Action Concerning Children in Armed Conflict.

1992: Committee on the Rights of the Child agrees to QUNO request for Day of General Discussion on children in armed conflict, and recommends a protocol to the Convention to raise the age for recruitment and use in hostilities to 18 years, in line with the Convention's definition of 'the child', and requests the UN Secretary General to undertake a high-level study on the issue.

Numerous resolutions in the UN Commission on Human Rights and General Assembly.

1993–1996: UN Study on the Impact of Armed Conflict on Children (Graça Machel); QUNO commissioned to do child soldier research for it, published as *Children: The invisible soldiers*. UN Study leads to creation of post of Special Representative of the UN Secretary General for Children and Armed Conflict.

1998: Coalition to Stop the Use of Child Soldiers formed. Rome Statute of the International Criminal Court includes as a war crime recruitment and use in hostilities of children under 15 years.

1999: International Labour Organisation (ILO) Convention 182 concerning the Prohibition and Immediate Action for the Elimination of the Worst Forms of Child Labour adopted with provision prohibiting forced labour of under-18s including "forced or compulsory recruitment of children for use in armed conflict".

2000: Optional Protocol on Involvement of Children in Armed Conflict adopted, setting 18 as minimum age for all recruitment and use in hostilities, except for voluntary recruitment into government armed forces, which is raised to at least 16.

Special Representative of the UN Secretary General on Children and Armed Conflict created, leading to action, further publications, and UN Security Council resolutions creating a Security Council Working Group and Monitoring and Reporting Mechanism.

2003–2004: QUNO's research, *Voices of girl child soldiers* (New York) and *Young soldiers: Why they choose to fight* (Geneva: ILO).

Ducking and weaving

A perennial problem for QUNO is finding that for one reason or another progress is blocked on our issues. Sometimes this may entail waiting out the blockages, for example the years of waiting for the political circumstances to change in order to make progress on conscientious objection to military service at the Commission on Human Rights (see p. 27).

However, it is also important to consider how to create opportunities, including by finding alternative routes. On child soldiers, the main block in the negotiations on the protocol to the Convention on the Rights of the Child came down to whether all under-18s should be protected from military recruitment and use. Within the ILO, forced labour of all under-18s was already prohibited. By moving the child soldier issue into the ILO, the question of minimum age was non-negotiable, and the issue became the scope of action to be prohibited.

With conscientious objection to military service, the initial effort to have a clear protection in the International Covenant on Civil and Political Rights failed, and the first attempt to persuade the Human Rights Committee to interpret the right to freedom of thought, conscience and religion as protecting conscientious objection also failed. This seemed to have blocked that route, and so it was followed by repeated attempts to get a resolution in the Commission on Human Rights but with little success. In fact, the breakthrough came when QUNO New York drafted and helped to negotiate a resolution at the UN General Assembly on "Status of persons refusing service in military or police forces used to enforce apartheid".[15] This enabled QUNO Geneva to follow up with a Commission resolution requesting a Sub-Commission Study on the whole subject of conscientious objection to military service. In turn, and with the change in the Cold War political circumstances, a succession of progressively stronger Commission resolutions became possible. However, in parallel, the Human Rights Committee's interpretation of the International Covenant on Civil and Political Rights was slowly evolving. This was the result of a number of factors,[16] not least QUNO's role in using the Commission resolutions to move the Committee forward, and then the Committee developments to strengthen the Commission resolutions. The end result was that the Committee reached the point at which, in 2006 in the case of *Yeo-Bum Yoon and Myung-Jin Choi v Republic of Korea*, it decisively ruled that conscientious objection to military service is protected under the Covenant provision on thought, conscience and religion.[17]

QUNO had worked with the conscientious objection movement in Republic of Korea (South Korea) over many years and, when this particular case was rejected by their Supreme and Constitutional Courts, encouraged and assisted them to submit the case to the Committee, since from the international perspective this was the ideal case we had been waiting for in order to enable the Committee to demonstrate its change of position. Ironically, the earlier negative position of the Human Rights Committee was based on the interpretation of the European Convention on Human Rights, and, in 2010, QUNO (together with four of our NGO partners) submitted an *amicus curiae* brief to the European Court of Human Rights largely based on the Human Rights Committee's case law, to seek to reverse the negative European jurisprudence! In July 2011, the Grand Chamber of the European Court[18] duly followed the Human Rights Committee's approach, thus for the first time creating a binding legal judgement that conscientious objection to military service is protected under the right to freedom of thought, conscience and religion, as well as establishing specifically that it is protected under the European Convention on Human Rights.

Facilitation

At one stage I was regularly invited to attend and address Ministerial Meetings of the Human Security Network.[19] This seemed absurd – to be flown halfway round the world in order to have ten minutes in which to speak on a subject. On the other hand, to have the undivided attention of a dozen foreign ministers and their closest advisers even for that length of time seemed too good an opportunity to miss. But more puzzling was: Why was I repeatedly invited? Of course, in part it was to do with the issues, but in the end my conclusion was that I had been appointed as a kind of Court Jester for the group: the person who could make them laugh while saying things that most of them would not have dared to say to each other. As Tony Stoller explains, "Medieval kings kept jesters by them, a Fool allowed licence to tell them the uncomfortable truth without (usually) suffering the standard penalty of the messenger bringing bad news."[20]

More generally, the ability of QUNO to 'tell it as it is' is important: whether by challenging attitudes and behaviour – for example, during discussions on extending weapons restrictions to civil (internal) wars pointing out that those governments arguing against it were in effect claiming the right to use weapons against their own people that they were prohibited from using on others; or, in off-the-record meetings at Quaker House, enabling others to speak frankly by being the one identifying the problematic countries, individual diplomats or issues; and often by using humour, such as suggesting that the statements by high-level government dignitaries would be enhanced by them having to wear a lie detector.

A factor that needs to be borne in mind if QUNO is to continue its role as a speaker of critical truths is the question of financial independence. If QUNO were to become too reliant on government funding, or funding from others who would not be willing to accept criticism, this could impact negatively on QUNO's work. The solid core of Quaker funding is QUNO's safeguard for its real independence from pressure or self-censorship in this regard.

Facilitating discussion on issues which may not be our own specific priorities arises in many different contexts. Sometimes it is a case of facilitating the work of other Quakers, such as the work on the rights of indigenous peoples where QUNO has supported the engagement of Canadian Friends Service Committee (CFSC) in the substantive work, and has also become recognised as a place where indigenous peoples can engage informally and constructively with government representatives. As one indigenous person put it, "Quaker House is the only place where both indigenous peoples and governments feel safe". Most recently, following the adoption of the UN Declaration on the Rights of Indigenous Peoples, Quaker House meetings enabled indigenous representatives to discuss amongst themselves what kind of mechanism of the new Human Rights Council they would like and then to present this to a group of governments, which led to the creation of the Expert Mechanism on the Rights of Indigenous Peoples (EMRIP) in a form closely resembling the indigenous proposal. After its creation, tensions arose about the operation of the EMRIP, and QUNO again hosted informal off-the-record discussions between the members of the Expert Mechanism and governments in order to clear the air and develop greater confidence on both sides leading to a significant improvement in the course of a couple of years.

A different kind of facilitation has been when a Quaker body in one country would like to access the UN. This may entail QUNO explaining the process and possibilities, submitting documents on behalf of the body, providing support and access for Quaker delegates, and/or organising events at Quaker House or elsewhere, for example for indigenous representatives supported by Australian Quakers when Australia was reporting under the International Convention on the Elimination of Racial Discrimination (see Box 1, p. 22). An example in the other direction has been the long-standing work between QUNO and CFSC in relation to the US conscientious objectors seeking asylum in Canada, where QUNO's expertise on the issues and UN contacts were shared with CFSC and the lawyers working on the cases.

Our contacts with government representatives arise because of our year-round presence and work on a range of issues and more general engagement with the UN human rights and refugee system as part of our general support for the UN and efforts to improve it. Since QUNO's main role is to bring about change on issues, we focus on trying to influence governments and the UN and its associated bodies, rather than involvement with other NGOs and NGO committees. Where we work with other NGOs is when this is useful for furthering our issues. However, this means that QUNO has access to government contacts and an understanding of UN processes which many other NGOs do not. So, for example, through organising Quaker House meetings inviting both the relevant NGOs and government representatives, QUNO was able to assist the NGOs working on the rights of persons with disabilities to get a UNHCR Executive Committee Conclusion about refugees with disabilities.[21]

Empowering other NGOs in this way is one of the contributions that QUNO can make, always of course within the limits of our time and resources. Similarly, QUNO's convening power is valued by NGO, UN and governmental representatives when they would like to be able to explore issues. Thus QUNO was asked to organise discussions about climate change and displacement in order to help others to brainstorm, discuss freely and start identifying what the issues might be and which of these are different from displacement caused by, or related to, other factors. This also enabled QUNO to start learning and thinking about these issues and eventually led, in response to Quaker concerns about climate change, to further work once QUNO was able to identify both an opportunity and a gap which we could contribute to addressing. In this instance, one of the points which QUNO identified was that little attention was being given to those who did not move, and to the communities who received those moving or displaced, as compared with those actually displaced or choosing to move, and ensured that these dimensions were also included in the thinking around the issues.

In other cases, it is what I would call the Falstaff syndrome, with QUNO being "the cause that wit is in other men" (as Shakespeare put it[22]), rather than being a main player in any form. It may be a case that discussions are blocked, or not taking place, and that QUNO may be able to help break the deadlock by organising informal, off-the-record discussions with some or all of the parties. Sometimes such efforts work; sometimes not. Or it may be that we know that Quakers are concerned about an issue or a situation and, even though we do not ourselves have specific proposals or insights, wish to encourage others who are, or perhaps should be, working in the area.

Complementarity of activities and working with others

Although so far I have contrasted QUNO's approach with that of some other NGOs, often in fact there is a need for both advocacy and facilitation rather than one or the other. This is parallel to the debates amongst Quakers about advocacy versus engagement with decision-makers. Sometimes in NGO strategy meetings where tasks are being agreed and parcelled out – "QUNO will do its thing" is the shorthand used for organising our informal, off-the-record lunch discussions. In my experience there has been increasing recognition by other human rights NGOs over recent years of the value of such meetings. At an earlier stage there had been misunderstandings or concerns about our 'hugger-mugger' or 'secretive' approach, with suspicions that we were betraying or undermining the position of other NGOs.

A different kind of complementarity can arise where, although we are working on a mutual objective with a government, either they are not yet ready to publicly commit to it, or to do so would be likely to lead to negative reactions from other governments. QUNO can then be the organiser of the 'side event' during the Human Rights Council session, or can propose a particular course of action. Another benefit of QUNO's acting can be that when we organise a Quaker House meeting, we decide who to invite or not to invite. If those not invited learn of the meeting, QUNO takes responsibility (and justifies our decisions). This can avoid diplomatic incidents or enable others to participate free from pressure from, for example, heavyweight governments within their own regional group. Similarly, we can be the public face or advocate of good ideas from within UN secretariats who are meant to be neutral or humanitarian, and thus may be hampered from putting forward proposals themselves.

There are many different longer term ways in which QUNO has worked with others. Some of these have been other NGOs; for example, the creation of the Coalition to Stop the use of Child Soldiers together with Amnesty International, Human Rights Watch, Jesuit Refugee Service, Save the Children Alliance and International Federation Terre des Hommes, formalised what was already a working partnership in seeking to get the Optional Protocol to the Convention on the Rights of the Child on involvement of children in armed conflict. This also gave rise to different examples of complementarity of approaches. Sometimes the Coalition was able to do or say things which not all its member NGOs could; sometimes it was agreed that a specific NGO would do something in its own name which was an essential element of the broader agreed strategy.

Sometimes it is an ongoing but informal collaboration, for example on conscientious objection to military service with, at the international level, War Resisters' International and, more recently, Conscience and Peace Tax International, and the European Bureau on Conscientious Objection (EBCO) at the regional level, and with local organisations such as New Profile in Israel, and the conscientious objector movements in Republic of Korea and Colombia. Here QUNO's role tends to be the international law and UN aspects, including diplomatic contacts, although in fact in all three of these countries there was also a Quaker element at times – in Israel with one of the ecumenical accompaniers, and in the other two with Quaker International Affairs Representatives of the American Friends Service Committee (AFSC).

The work on women in prison developed a joint project group comprising representatives of QUNO, the Quaker Council for European Affairs (QCEA), the FWCC representatives to the UN Commission on Crime Prevention and Criminal Justice (Vienna) and QPSW, and the meetings of this group have continued because of its value in sharing information and considering future action even after the focus had shifted from women prisoners specifically to a broader criminal justice/prisoners agenda. In the course of our work on women prisoners and children of prisoners, QUNO developed links with Quakers in India, Kyrgyzstan, USA and elsewhere, as well as with Penal Reform International and the Mary Knoll Sisters in Brazil, and many others. The external evaluation of this work highlighted the way

> QUNO mobilised its existing relationships with other NGOs, thus basing its action on mutual understanding and trust, and added new contacts as far as useful and possible. The partners unanimously praised the pragmatic, flexible and effective approach of QUNO when talking about cooperation and division of tasks, avoiding unnecessary formalism.[23]

Working with others may have as its primary focus achieving the specific objective, such as a new UN standard or procedure, and/or the wish to involve others so that if we do our job well enough, they will take up 'our' causes because they are persuaded and so take them on as their own. For example, child soldiers was originally only QUNO, together with the International Committee of the Red Cross, the Swedish and Icelandic Red Cross Societies and Swedish Save the Children (Rädda Barnen), but now there is a broad range of UN, government and NGO actors, and so QUNO has moved on to other issues, although Quakers in different countries and organisations are still actively involved.

Being present

> The work occupies a great deal of the time of the Centre staff … It does not happen at a specific time or on a particular day; it goes on all the time and it has to be entrusted to a person or persons specially appointed for the purpose because it requires continuous attention and a background of experience.[24]

It is not only that QUNO staff build strong contacts, and are able to identify potential opportunities, or respond to specific requests, because we are there – in and around the UN, and at Quaker House – but also sometimes simply being visibly present can be important, even when we have nothing specific to say or do. This arises in a number of different ways, including being there to hear victims of human rights violations speaking about their experiences, or when a government's record is being examined by a UN human rights body. Recently a diplomat thanked me for attending his government's quizzing by the Human Rights Committee! On another occasion, I mentioned to the head of the government delegation, with whom I had worked over many years, the question I would have asked if I had been a member of the Committee on the Rights of the Child, and in his responses to the Committee, he responded to the "unasked" question!

Of course, mere presence is not enough:

> Expertise: QUNO has already a strong position in the field of human rights within the UN context, its previous work on this field being fully recognised by the various partners, experts and decision-making bodies. QUNO started implementing the project with a good level of expertise on the specific issues of the project, and managed to extend and deepen this expertise in close interaction with the partners and stakeholders.[25]

However, if we are not present and engaged on a regular basis, it is difficult to know what is on the minds of our interlocutors and to build relationships. "Relations with other international organisations cannot, and should not, be confined to pure business: they are bound also to include much discussion and exchange of views and they naturally become personal as well as official."[26]

Being visibly present can be a challenge for an organisation much of whose work is done behind the scenes. Different QUNO programmes and representatives have approached this in various ways. In the Human Rights & Refugees programme, it was one of the reasons I decided to continue a practice developed by my predecessor, Martin Macpherson, of publishing an annual report on the UN Commission on Human Rights and, subsequently, on the UN Human Rights Council. These publications gave us high visibility and standing amongst the diplomatic, NGO and human rights communities, as engaged, informed and supportively critical observers, as well as providing a platform to highlight our own issues and developments on them, and to float ideas to improve things many of which have been adopted by governments or other NGOs as their own. Having such a high profile publication has made many people (both in and around the UN and elsewhere) aware of QUNO, its existence, activities and issues, and has also, therefore, served as a means for disseminating our views and more specific publications but also as an entrée with new government representatives and others.

Timescale

One of the hallmarks of Quaker UN work is the willingness to commit for the duration. It is difficult for governments and NGOs to sustain long-term commitment. This is one of the significant differences between QUNO and others. Work on conscientious objection to military service *at the UN* (obviously work on the issue elsewhere has been going on for much longer!) started in 1950, and QUNO achieved its objective of legal recognition of it as a right 56 years later. Work on child soldiers started in 1979, and 2009 was the first year in which it ceased to be listed amongst QUNO's human rights priorities (though again, Quaker work in different places continues). By contrast, QUNO 'only' took up the issue of women in prison in 2003 and had achieved its major objectives by 2010.

The question of the long-term commitment is important. It highlights the centrality of careful discernment, by staff and committees, of the issues to take up since we may be committing for twenty or even fifty years. This also means that, even with the relatively long terms of many Quaker representatives to the UN, one individual often will not see an issue through from beginning to end. The dedication of individual staff to sustain work at issues that may not be achieved, or at least not on their watch, and where setbacks and frustrations may be more evident than progress, to be constantly looking for new channels or approaches to try to move things along, not only requires certain skills and character traits but also a supportive environment from the Quaker UN Committees in particular but also from Quakers more generally.

Failures

It may sound as though everything that QUNO does is a success, but this is, of course, not true. Obviously, more is heard of the successes – partly because there is more to say, and not only because it is pleasanter to talk about success than failure, but failure is important. If we did not have failures, it is likely that we would not be trying things that we should be trying. Certainly, in my experience, some of our successes were not foregone conclusions when we tried them. The opportunity to try things which may not work is a vital part of QUNO's role. The opportunity to fail needs to be safeguarded. In an often donor-driven environment, there is a tendency either to be sufficiently cautious in objectives and activities to make failure unlikely, or to mask failures in order to be able to report on how successful the organisation or programme is. This is understandable, though regrettable, but makes it even more important that QUNO can experiment and 'give it a try', secure in the knowledge that in itself failure is not a disgrace. Of course, failure needs to be looked at, both to ensure that it was not due to lack of or inappropriate preparation or activity, and also to learn why it did not work and how these findings can be taken on board in other activities.

Failures are of different kinds. Some failures arise from a brave attempt that does not work, because people are not willing to engage and we are unable to find a way to engage them. For example, QUNO made several attempts to organise Quaker House lunch discussions about the Durban Racism Review Conference,[27] but was unable to get support for these from the government representatives who would be needed in order to make it worthwhile. Sometimes it is because we try to draw in people who are incapable, unwilling or unable to participate in our kind of informal off-the-record discussions. Sometimes it is because of trying to stretch a group too far beyond its comfort zone, and so people decline to come, or come but do not really engage.

Other kinds of failures arise from omissions – a lack of vision, or failure to grasp an opportunity. It may be a lack of resources or of specific capacities in the QUNO staff – too many demands on a small staff meaning a timely opportunity is lost, or language limitations, or lack of an important contact or of substantive background, or lack of funding or other resources – such as competition for the use of Quaker House itself. Sometimes it is a failure of strategy – was the child soldier strategy flawed, or would the result have been the same whatever we did? We had wanted a complete prohibition on any recruitment or use in combat of under-18-year-olds, but ended up with a provision allowing continued recruitment of 'volunteers' into government armed forces from 16, although with safeguards and pressure to raise that age, and at least 23 states have done so in law or policy. Sometimes it is a failure of results because the decisions are not ours to make. In the end, it is the government representatives who negotiate and adopt resolutions and treaties.

But it is also important to remember that many failures are or can be turned into temporary setbacks on the road to success. Often it is a question of accepting reverses and trying to figure another route to our objective. Writing in April 1973, Duncan Wood (then Director of the QUNO, Geneva) described 'The Debacle' in relation to the attempt to get a resolution on conscientious objection to military service in the UN Commission on Human Rights, when the USSR moved and won a motion to postpone the item to the following year, concluding, "those who oppose militarism and violent solutions to human problems have a long uphill struggle still before them".[28] In 1977, he commented, "In this matter there is still no progress to report: neither at its 32nd Session in 1976, nor at its 33rd in 1977, did the Commission on Human Rights find the time to deal effectively with the subject."[29] Many of the succeeding QUNO staff could report in similar terms of efforts frustrated on this issue, before the eventual breakthrough with a resolution in 1987. The biggest difference then was the shift of the USSR towards *glasnost*, but if Quakers and others had not done the groundwork and persisted during the intervening period, they would not have been ready and able to take advantage of the opening when it came. It is important not to forget nor to minimise the years during which QUNO maintained its commitment to and work on this issue, never knowing whether or when there would be a breakthrough, and fielding disappointment after disappointment. The fact that we can look back now, knowing that success would be achieved, means that we owe even more to those who toiled apparently fruitlessly during the previous years.

A similar example of an initial setback was the work on women in prison. The first approach by QUNO in 2003 was through the (then) UN Sub-Commission on the Promotion and Protection of Human Rights which responded enthusiastically; but the resulting document was disappointing. QUNO therefore switched track, publishing its own research[30] and pursuing other more productive lines, but this was also the start of a new approach by QUNO of research and publishing in order to explore and publicise the issues, drawing on the interest and talents of the various programme assistants.

Casting bread upon the waters

Some of QUNO's work is providing 'good ideas'. Because of the longevity and commitment, and the quiet listening and analysing of what is going on, QUNO is sometimes in a position to provide not only analysis but proposals. Many of these are quite technical, and so do not garner a lot of attention or interest outside 'Geneva circles'. For example, the practice of governments issuing standing invitations to the UN's human rights Special Procedures was my idea (a rare 'light bulb' moment of inspiration) for addressing the problem faced in getting agreement to visit countries. 'Special Procedures' (see also glossary pp. 92–3) are independent human rights experts who can only visit countries if invited to do so by the government. By getting prior consent through a standing invitation to all Special Procedures to visit, one of the obstacles could be eliminated or reduced (at least in principle). In this instance, after a delay, the idea was acted upon by the government of Norway, which enabled QUNO and other NGOs to then start working on other governments, and eventually it became part of the policy of some governments to encourage others to issue such invitations.[31]

Often we propose ideas, or actions, and never know – or only discover later – that these have been taken up. This is separate from the difficulty of 'proving' cause and effect, such as the example of sealing the Central Records Office in Pristina in order to preserve the records of Kosovan Albanians who had been expelled (see pp. 31–32). Sometimes I am credited with things of which I have no recollection – is this because they were simply not memorable or significant enough to me, or because indeed I am being given credit for others' achievements? Certainly on occasions it is because of something that one of my colleagues or other Quakers have done, and so it is really Quakers or QUNO who are being credited rather than the specific individual: for example, abolishing slavery or being involved in the Ottawa Treaty to ban landmines.

QUNO as a 'privileged interlocutor'

One of the reasons why QUNO is heard and listened to is that we have built credibility by the work we do on specific issues. Others know that the issues on which we work are well-grounded, not trendy, not superficial, and so people respect it, even if they do not agree – indeed our 'good opinion' is often sought because it cannot be bought and is not given if we do not feel it is deserved! But equally, building those contacts – with individuals representing governments and working in the various UN and international secretariats, with NGOs, and with experts, and rebuilding the new contacts as the specific individuals rotate out of Geneva or move to new positions, means that when we need such contacts, as in the Kosovo example, we are likely to have them (though inevitably this is not always the case). Many of the relationships thus built are enduring ones – often returning diplomats make contact to reconnect, or indeed maintain contact in their new postings, whether in their own capital or elsewhere. This network can be beneficial for the broader Quaker work as key partnerships may develop by linking QUNO contacts with other Quakers or Quaker work.

In this way the different strands and kinds of QUNO work are *complementary*. In my experience you cannot build contacts without substance. It is because we work on issues that we build the contacts with the different individuals and groups. Equally, although there may be tensions between our work as *facilitators* enabling discussions to take place and as *advocates* of specific issues or positions, they are not mutually exclusive, at least most of the time. On the other hand, I am aware that there are times when I feel that we 'got it wrong', when we became too much or the wrong kind of advocates during some of the work on child soldiers and not only limited our role as facilitators but also limited our effectiveness in forwarding the child soldier issue by being 'boxed in'. Looking back, it is always easy to criticise (in particular to be self-critical) while it is impossible to know whether doing things differently would have produced better results. Even at the time, it was clear that QUNO was identified as having a position of opposing any under-18-year-olds being in armed forces as well as their being involved in actual fighting. For QUNO it was clear that the prohibition on fighting alone would not be adequate to actually prevent 'children' being used or exposed to attack. However, this meant that with regard to those governments strongly and vocally opposing such a complete ban there was little or no opportunity to engage in discussion. It is possible that if the research on child soldiers had been done first and we had engaged the governments in the learning process about the realities of the situations and the impact on the children, that more of the 'opposing' governments might have been persuaded to soften their position. This was one of the 'lessons learned' carried forward into the work on women in prison and children of prisoners – to constantly share with the governments what we were learning while we were learning it, and thus to seek to build their understanding and engagement with the issues before any question of a standard-setting exercise arose.

Expecting the unexpected

The need for proper planning, testing, approval and reporting on work is unquestioned. At the same time, there is a need to build in enough flexibility to enable QUNO to take advantage of the opportunities that occur unexpectedly. A recent and very positive example was the Thai initiative to create new UN Rules for the Treatment of Women Prisoners and Non-Custodial Measures for Women Offenders (the Bangkok Rules). We had no forewarning of this specific initiative although we had been involved in the research and activities which created the momentum for it. It was not in the QUNO workplan for 2009, but clearly it was what we wanted and it would have made no sense if we had not engaged fully in the drafting, promotion and advocacy for these new Rules.

Holding the faith

As we have already seen, one of the hallmarks of QUNO work is the willingness to stick with issues for the long-term. One of the corollaries of this is that often QUNO is not 'trendy' – this year's issue may be Z, while QUNO continues to work on A. At times, this may make QUNO seem 'out of step', but often the underlying issues remain the same, even if the particular manifestation of them is different. 'Ethnic cleansing' was no different in essence from other forms of racism, discrimination or genocide, all of which have common roots, and any of which can be exploited and encouraged in order to achieve particular ends. In a sense this can be seen as one of the contemporary challenges, as well as one of the perennial ones. Today in Europe, the labelling and concomitant exclusion from full human status and therefore human rights protection may relate more to irregular migrants and asylum-seekers than to slaves. However, what is unchanging is the need for and rightness of Quakers' work not only to ameliorate the conditions of those treated in this way, but to challenge the government and public policies and perceptions under which people are so treated. QUNO and its work on human rights at the UN is one avenue through which this can be done. One of the benefits which the UN approach can bring to the national/ domestic scene is that, once adopted and applicable, UN human rights standards continue to apply, and it is harder for governments to go back on them. An excellent example of this is the work on the abolition of the death penalty, which has advanced to the stage that when, immediately post-9/11, some European politicians called for the reintroduction of the death penalty, the simple response was that this was not possible because of their international and European human rights obligations.

By contrast, the USA's deliberate undermining of the prohibition on torture, although to some extent held in check through the UN human rights mechanisms, did significant damage to their normative value as well as encouraging the justification of such practices in a number of countries in addition to the USA itself. If the international standards and UN mechanisms had not been in place, it is possible that the work done to outlaw torture would have been even more severely damaged, and the US actions become accepted as the norm rather than an aberration.

And darkness was on the face of the deep

The regression and challenge post-9/11 (not only in relation to torture) has been one of the most marked setbacks during my time at QUNO. Nevertheless, it highlighted at least two things: first, how much worse things could have been without the international standards; second, that the basic, unglamorous building-blocks of robust, independent judicial processes, and the rule of law more generally, are one of the best protections for the most vulnerable in all times, including during emergencies and times of fear. As Quakers learned, their own freedom to protest – not only that of 'others' – was under threat from counter-terrorism legislation and police action.

During this period, one of the things that QUNO did was to provide a confidential space where individuals from different parts of the 'human rights community' in Geneva could come together for mutual support and to discuss and brainstorm during a very bleak time.

Neutrality

A common fallacy (in my view) is about Quaker neutrality. It comes up in a number of different ways. In relation to organising informal, off-the-record meetings there is a tendency to refer to the Quaker Houses as 'neutral'. There is an element of truth in this because we are 'neutral between the participants', in the sense that we are not politically aligned – whether it is between different governments, different regional groups or blocs, or between governments and non-governmental organisations. In this sense, QUNO is neutral in that we do not favour one over the other because of who they are. This aspect of 'neutrality' is important.

Sometimes we may be 'neutral' on issues when there is actually no Quaker position on them, but this is much rarer and has tended to come up more in relation to some of the trade issues than human rights. I am not neutral on torture, or the death penalty, or sending kids into combat. I am, however, willing to discuss these issues with anyone, and to facilitate discussions on them. However, if, at a Quaker House lunch, the discussion were to start moving towards support for any of these, I would not hesitate to intervene – although none of these have, to my recollection occurred, there have been occasions when I did feel that the discussion was not heading in a direction that would help to enhance the promotion and protection of human rights, and said so by putting counter arguments. This did not appear to deter any of the participants from accepting the next invitation to Quaker House!

Sometimes we may be 'neutral' on specifics while being clear about process (such as the importance of involvement of all concerned parties in developing the result) or about the values involved. It is, therefore, important to distinguish between our values, on which we are not and should not be neutral, and our approach to others. Around the UN, ideas are often rejected because of the political quarter from which they have come. Being willing to look at each idea or position on its own merits is one of the attributes of Quaker UN work. One result of this is precisely our ability to work with governments from different regions and political backgrounds, as well as to engage with those governments themselves on good and not so good aspects of their behaviour. In my experience, no government is wholly good or wholly bad in relation to human rights.

QUNO's perceived lack of political alignment, together with its recognised expertise and trustworthiness, has also led to its advice and assistance being sought by many delegations from different regions. Sometimes it is on purely technical points – for example, "When was the first resolution on X adopted?" or "How does Y happen?" Part of this is understanding that many of those being asked to work on human rights or refugee issues are not specialists in the subject, and therefore being happy to fill gaps in knowledge without making the questioner feel stupid. Sometimes it is linguistic assistance – checking the draft of a resolution before it is sent back to capital, or a quick pronunciation lesson for difficult English words before a statement has to be delivered! Small things in themselves, but indicative both of the kind of relationship that can develop, and sometimes of an opportunity to suggest additional or different points or ideas for inclusion.

Much of this kind of work will never be known. Partly this is because the nature of relationship was such that QUNO's role was not acknowledged, and for QUNO, having the idea taken on was the objective, not getting credit for ourselves. Indeed, more generally, this is part of the QUNO approach – making progress on the issue is what is important and if that means a government getting the credit, so be it. This can create tensions when demonstrating QUNO's 'effectiveness' whether for our Quaker constituency or for donors. Why fund an organisation that cannot show results? But, if claiming results undermines the likelihood of replicating them…

The challenge of Quaker UN work

It might be assumed that QUNO is so well-established that it is easy for new staff to step into the work but, in my view, this would be a mistake. Yes, an ongoing programme may enable a new staff member to undertake activities and follow the QUNO 'house style' as it were. However, it is also essential for each staff member to make the work their own – to understand and draw from that understanding the nature, purpose and specific activities and approaches for their part in the work. Without such understanding, the form may remain, but it will be built on sand rather than rock, and may well lose its efficacy or direction. Thus it is not just that each staff member does the work differently because they bring their own skills and methods of work. At the same time, it can be daunting to take on the mantle of Quaker UN work because of QUNO and its staff's reputations and the weight of expectations.

There is also the constant challenge of keeping the work within bounds – it is hard to walk away from issues to take days off when we are deeply engaged with them. When we were negotiating the child soldiers Protocol, I was aware that many of the government representatives were going home to watch the Winter Olympics, whilst I was having nightmares about the child soldiers and their families. Equally, the opportunities for Quaker UN work are so prolific, and the amount of lobbying we receive to have QUNO involved, means that constant restraint is required if we are not to be overwhelmed.

An important component in the work, and in the training of future QUNO and related staff, are the programme assistants. Many of these young people have brought extraordinary skills and vision to the work, contributing significantly to its development and implementation, in particular to the human rights work by their research and publications on women in prison and children of prisoners, as well as their technical expertise, logistical skills in arranging side events and Quaker House lunches, and interpersonal skills with diplomats, indigenous people, local NGO activists and others.

Relationship between Quaker UN work and other Quaker work and activities

Sometimes, Friends seem to view Quaker work at the UN as some kind of pinnacle – 'stalking the corridors of power hobnobbing with important people'. The reality can be very different. But, furthermore, it must never be forgotten that QUNO's reputation, credibility and input rests largely on the work of other Quakers. QUNO did not 'dream up' the work on conscientious objection or women prisoners. These are issues based on the long-standing and continuing concerns and work of Quakers in many different countries.

There is a danger that QUNO are seen as 'the experts', and that the work is so esoteric and rarefied that it does not really relate to the lived reality of most Quakers. Although some of the arcane UN processes – should it be the Committee or the Commission for this issue at this point? – and the consequent strategy may perhaps be left to QUNO, to 'leave it to QUNO' more generally would be to undermine the work, both because of the need for it to be built on a solid foundation and because the UN is usually only one element in promoting change. Much work needs to be done within individual countries to create change, and even in the UN work, because so much of the UN is dictated or negotiated by governments, having people within countries making their concerns and requests known to their government can be crucial.

At times there has also been useful reinforcement between the European and UN levels, with the Quaker Council for European Affairs (QCEA) acting, for example, on conscientious objection to military service or following up on the work on women prisoners through the European institutions, as well as between QUNO Geneva and QUNO New York (for example, the two QUNOs undertook some specific research on girl soldiers), and, of course, there is the example of the UN General Assembly CO/apartheid resolution which not only fulfilled its direct purpose of giving quasi-refugee status to the young men leaving South Africa because of their refusal to serve in the armed forces but also opened the way for progress in Geneva on the general issue of conscientious objection to military service.

CHAPTER 6

Conclusion:
Looking back – looking forward

God, grant me the serenity to accept the things I cannot change, the courage to change the things I can, and the wisdom to know the difference.

(Reinhold Niebuhr, 1892–1971)

Does this exploration of Quaker UN work on human rights lead to any conclusions?

Looking back

I am, of course, not an impartial observer, but from my experience it is clear that Quakers can make a difference through the UN.

What QUNO has done

We have been involved in identifying issues and putting them on the international agenda, creating new international standards and processes to address them, and seeing real change as a result. This does not mean that the problems are solved – there are still child soldiers, there are still countries in which conscientious objection to military service is not recognised and in which too many women are sent to prison – but in many instances, QUNO has created tools which are being and can continue to be used to keep trying to improve the situation.

Perhaps even more significant has been the change in attitudes. For example, it is hard now to believe that it was only in 1999 during the European Conference to Stop the Use of Child Soldiers that it became clear that amongst European governments the attitude had shifted to the point that they no longer considered it acceptable to send under-18s into combat. The value of maintaining the persistent struggle to change attitudes and not only law cannot, in my view, be over-emphasised.

As we have seen with the regression on some issues, such as torture, laws can be changed or reinterpreted, or ignored, but if we can actually get people to understand and accept the rightness of our perceptions, they will not want or accept such reversions.

This is not to minimise the value of laws: on the contrary, the process of creation of new standards can be part of the education and convincement activities, and equally, law – however weak the enforcement measures of international law – has its own value both as the standard and also to provide protection for individuals and continued pressure on recalcitrant governments. Without legal standards on torture, there would only have been the moral and practical arguments to raise, and the UN and other governments would have found it harder to keep the pressure on the USA and its partners that what they were doing in the wake of 9/11 was unlawful as well as immoral. Equally, without the European-wide ban on the death penalty it is possible that it might have been reintroduced in some countries. At the UK domestic level, would the courts have been able to hold the line to the extent that they did without the Human Rights Act?

More specifically in relation to the human rights issues on which QUNO has worked, it is important to reflect that each issue was valid in its own right as based on fundamental Quaker understandings and beliefs about the value of the individual. At the same time, each has enabled at least an entry into broader discussion. For example, the work on child soldiers and on conscientious objection to military service, though both specific in focus, have raised issues about the nature and role of armed forces in society and challenged government assumptions about the legitimacy of demands for participation in the military. The work on women in prison and children of prisoners has addressed the specifics of the situation faced by each of these groups, but has also enabled renewed discussions on the over-use of prison as a response to crime, as well as attitudes both to individuals who commit crimes and to their families. Direct approaches on these kinds of issues would have been unlikely to gain a hearing because punitive attitudes are so entrenched and visceral. In addition, all the above issues, as well as the work on torture and the death penalty, engage Quaker insights about the value of each individual life, personality and conscience and the capacity of every individual to change.

The UN is subject to many criticisms, many of them justified. At the same time, if we value dialogue and discussion and efforts to promote these, we need to beware of being overly critical of the 'talking shop' aspect of the UN. To change attitudes requires the ability to exchange views and often over protracted periods of time. QUNO's major contributions in this area are to use the opportunities presented to introduce new ideas, or to continue working on long-established ones, through UN processes but also to complement them through our own informal, off-the-record meetings which are designed to enable a more profound exchange of views and introduction of new ideas. In that sense, we are a facilitator and process-player as well as a substantive actor on issues.

Finally, by using the UN multilateral system and demonstrating our long-term commitment to it, we are also validating its principles despite the undoubted organisational flaws – the pursuit of peace and justice through discussion, negotiation and common endeavour rather than competition and force.

Is QUNO work different?

Is *Quaker* UN work on human rights different from that of other NGOs? In some respects, no: like many others we take up issues, we make written and oral statements to UN bodies, respond to requests for input to UN reports, engage in negotiations on resolutions and new international standards, and so on.

However, in process terms QUNO is certainly unusual if not unique as an NGO, in engaging so many parts of the UN system in order to make progress on our specific issues. Although this has challenges both in the amount of time required and in developing sufficient expertise in how to use the different systems, it has the benefit of creating opportunities and ways around obstructions which might not otherwise be available.

There is also, as previously stressed, the long-term nature of Quaker engagement, both with the UN in general and on our specific issues; the willingness to stick with an issue even in the face of apparent lack of progress over many years, until the time is right and movement is possible. This requires our constant presence, patience, persistence and constancy of purpose – as well as conviction that if we keep at it, at some point change is possible – while we continue to look for the different avenues and approaches that might create openings, and also try to identify the key elements. With some issues this is easier as it is an incremental process – which may seem slow and tedious, but at least gives the opportunity to remedy shortcomings or mistakes. With others, it is a one-off opportunity – or a second chance is unlikely at least for years – and getting all the pieces into place to ensure that the best chance is created requires thought, testing and sometimes the patience to wait – and wait. For many NGOs, the pressure for quick and demonstrable results may limit their capacity for this kind of long-term, inglorious and often behind-the-scenes role. It may also discourage them from taking up issues that are unlikely to be achievable within a year or two.

Looking forward

I have been asked to reflect on what might be some of the issues that Quakers should perhaps be addressing. Because I am who I am – a Quaker human rights lawyer – I shall limit myself to two areas where I believe it is essential that Quakers are engaged, and each of which is grounded in fundamental Quaker thought and practice. My identifying what I see as the underlying principles makes it clear that the examples given are only examples, are not exclusive, and are likely to change over time.

We are all human

One of the most profound Quaker insights, in my view, is the recognition not only of "that of God in every one" but the implications in terms of treating each person as a human being. This accords with the foundational discourse of human rights, the *inherent* nature of human rights in each individual, "without discrimination of any kind such as race, colour, sex, language, religion, political or other opinion, national or social origin, property, birth or other status", in the words of the 1948 Universal Declaration of Human Rights. It is also a vital challenge to the tendency of societies to exclude and scapegoat. This is not new, but it is certainly evident today and current manifestations of it should be central to Quaker belief and action.

We need to recognise both the common core that it is right and proper that Quakers address because of their beliefs, and also some of the current social trends. We need to ensure that no-one is labelled in a way that permits them to be stigmatised and treated as less than human. This means that we need to be alert to the use of terminology and the images it portrays, and the intent or unintended consequences of those terms and images.

Quakers have a long history of identifying the common humanity in unpopular or neglected groups – slaves (abolition of the slave trade and of slavery), women (right to vote and equality in marriage and ministry), the mentally ill (The Retreat), prisoners (Elizabeth Fry and many others), refugees (*Kindertransport*), those involved in wars (humanitarian relief to Germany after the First and Second World Wars), and so on. Unfortunately, many of these groups remain unpopular, marginalised or neglected – asylum-seekers and irregular migrants; prisoners; gay, lesbian, bisexual, transgender and intersex people; those with mental or physical disabilities; and the mentally ill; and there are contemporary forms of slavery (as well as more traditional forms still lurking).

The challenge is to maintain the insight and to keep looking, within ourselves and others, for the excluded, marginalised and disliked. To look with scepticism at all labelling of groups of people, since this is the easiest way to dehumanise, by eliminating the personal and individual, and creating images. Who is an *Islamic terrorist*? What image does this conjure up? And yet, I have had supper with some who are labelled thus. Who are the *drunken yobs* who disturb the peace and order of 'our' streets? Have you never, as a teenager or young adult, had a rowdy late night discussion in a public place? Who is the *murderer* who should be sent to prison for life? The woman prisoner I met who killed her father because he had just killed her boyfriend and was threatening to kill her?

Can we do everything and answer that of God in everyone – no. But we can constantly challenge prevailing assumptions, which are often based on ignorance, lack of thought, or deliberate manipulations to ensure the continued lack of sympathy and understanding. We all fall into the trap – on a lighter note, how often have I faced the "But Quakers are all dead, and they wear grey clothes, don't they?" reaction. Well, I don't think I'm dead (yet) and I don't very often wear grey.

It was the recognition of everyone as fellow human beings that led to the anti-slavery movement, and to action against the death penalty and torture. Equally, it has been the Quaker recognition of the common humanity of those held in prison and of those who seek asylum that has grounded and continues to ground this work. Quakers in Britain and elsewhere have made, and continue to make, a significant contribution both through individual acts, and humanitarian and other assistance, and through seeking to change policy and public perception in both these areas. Learning from the Mennonites in Canada, Quakers pioneered in Britain the work with released sex offenders through circles of support and accountability.

Clearly, these areas of work need to continue. In particular, both those who move across borders in an irregular fashion (and sometimes those who move legally), and those who come into conflict with the law, are currently amongst the most maligned. Equally, in Europe, this indubitably includes the Roma (gypsies/Sinti/Travellers).

The right to dissent

Quakers have a long tradition of accepting lawful authority, except where it conflicts with their conscientiously held beliefs, but even then accepting the lawful consequences of their acts. For many, from the earliest days through decades of conscientious objection to military service and more recent acts of civil disobedience, this has meant being willing to go to prison for their beliefs, not seeking to evade the consequences of their refusal to obey the law.

There is a need to counter the increasing invasion of government in ways that lead to increased social control, in particular through criminalisation and use of detention, and the fostering of insecurity and fear that permits and encourages such encroachments. The right to dissent, to be different, not to conform, are essential to individuality. As a society of 'dissenters' Quakers should be at the forefront in insisting on this not only for ourselves but for others, and not only in the traditional forms of protest and demonstration, in particular against government policies, but also against societal pressures to conformity. Individuals should be able to live their own lives in their own idiosyncratic way, with only the caveat that this does not cause harm to others.

The challenge is to keep the broadest space open for individual conscience. I do not think it is for me to decide or establish the limits, since this is a right of individual dissent – provided only that violence is neither used nor incited.

One of the areas Quakers might wish to explore is precisely what are the limits of government authority to dictate what people may or may not do. Here, it is important to maintain the distinction between providing the best information and advice to enable and encourage individuals to take or desist from certain actions, and the use of enforcement powers.[1]

One particular area is, of course, the use of conscription (obligatory/compulsory military service). This was not traditional in the UK, being introduced with great trepidation as an emergency measure in 1916, and reintroduced a few months before the outbreak of the Second World War. In many countries and by many people it is accepted that the government/state has the right to require military service of its citizens. I do not accept this and have sought to ensure that in all the work on conscientious objection to military service, QUNO has not endorsed this idea, but has simply put forward that if the state does this, there must be one or more alternatives "compatible with the reasons for the objection"[2] for those who object on grounds of conscience. This careful phrasing was designed to encompass not only those willing to undertake unarmed military service and those willing to undertake a civilian alternative service, but also those who believe that to undertake such work also supports or legitimises the military and/or the war effort, or who have a fundamental objection to state compulsion and therefore will not be part of it at all. Such a one was the distinguished Quaker scientist Kathleen Lonsdale, who went to prison rather than undertake compulsory fire-watching.[3] In 1945, British Quakers issued a statement setting out their reasons for opposing military conscription and urged its abolition, incidentally foreshadowing the future concern about child soldiers, pointing to the "effect on sensitive young minds".[4]

This is just one specific example, but there is also the issue of the privatisation of government functions and its consequences, in particular those areas linked to enforcement and restrictions on individual liberty and security, such as prisons and other detention centres. Should 'for profit' companies be given such powers, and what are the ethics – as well as the practical implications – of having such institutions run for profit?

Conclusion

My own experience and observation convinces me that Quakers have made a significant contribution in the human rights and refugee fields at the UN, and through the UN have helped to change attitudes, create new understandings, develop new standards and, through these processes, to make concrete and measurable changes in government policies and practices and in people's lives.

At its best, the work has been thoroughly grounded in Quaker understanding and insight, and has drawn on the work being done by Quakers and Quaker bodies in different countries. The pattern of individual and corporate concern leading to Quaker engagement on an issue at the UN, with new standards and procedures which are picked up and used in-country, is a strong one. When QUNO's activities are divorced from local or national action, they may be valid in their own right, but being without roots they may not be long-lasting or create real change. This is not just a question of QUNO taking up issues on which Friends are not themselves actively engaged, it can also be a case of 'leaving it to QUNO'. Equally, not all issues on which Friends are active or interested are most appropriately addressed through the UN.

The QUNO capacity to initiate action, draw in others, move things forward at and through the UN and other multilateral processes, and then step back when it is clear that this is now sufficiently mainstream within the UN, or when enough other organisations are actively engaged that the process is self-sustaining, is fundamental. Without it, success would be less likely, and the capacity to take up other issues hampered. At the same time, in itself, this constitutes clear evidence that ideas and attitudes have been taken on board by others, which is, after all, one of the objectives.

Finally, the recognition and value placed by others – government representatives, non-governmental organisations, human rights experts, UN staff and other secretariats – on the informal, off-the-record meetings organised by QUNO is unequivocal validation of this methodology. This is over and above the use of these to promote our specific priorities at any one time. It enables QUNO to assist others on a much broader range of issues, to engage actors who we might not otherwise be working with so actively, to facilitate access for others and also to enable discussions which might not otherwise take place – or not between these parties, or not in such a productive and open fashion.

It is challenging to be put in a position where the opportunities are seemingly so great. This carries responsibilities: to be wary of turning away from or not seeking out possibilities, while being alert to the need to maintain focus, and keeping space for creative exploration and lateral thinking as well as for rest! At the same time, the weight of responsibility and needs can be overwhelming.

The best I can do is echo the words of Duncan and Katharine Wood as they were leaving Geneva after their 25 years of Quaker service there:

> It may seem presumptuous to suppose that so insignificant a minority has anything of importance to contribute to the solution of the vast problems which beset humanity … but we leave Geneva convinced that the pioneers who came here to make a witness for Friends at the League were rightly guided and that all the tumultuous changes which have shaken our vision of the world have not shaken the foundation and validity of the Quaker faith.[5]

GLOSSARY

American Friends Service Committee (AFSC)

A Quaker organisation that includes people of various faiths who are committed to social justice, peace and humanitarian service. The work is based on the principles of the Religious Society of Friends, the belief in the worth of every person, and faith in the power of love to overcome violence and injustice.

Concern

In Quaker terminology, a concern is a spiritual leading which the individual cannot evade. Traditionally, an individual tests their leading through the formal structures of the Quaker bodies to ensure that it is a true leading rather than an enthusiasm or good idea. If endorsed, the concern may be acted on individually and/or corporately. As Christine Davis puts it in her Swarthmore Lecture, *Minding the Future*, "The concern takes on a life which is broader than the thoughts of the initiator: it feeds the originator as much as it is fed by that individual. We do not own our concerns; we are stewards of them. We take care of the work, and the work influences who we are."[1] She goes on, "Faithfulness to our testimonies rarely allows us to celebrate the completion of a task; for in some shape or form there will always be further work to be done. The nature of the work will depend largely upon the circumstances as well as upon the skills available for tackling them."

Ecumenical accompanier

The Ecumenical Accompaniment Programme in Palestine and Israel (EAPPI) is a World Council of Churches (WCC) initiative which was established in 2002 in response to a call made by the Heads of Churches in Jerusalem, and by Palestinian and Israeli NGOs. The mission of the EAPPI is to accompany Palestinians and Israelis in their nonviolent actions and concerted advocacy efforts to end the occupation.

Friend

Members of the Religious Society of Friends (Quakers) are known as Friends or Quakers. The latter was originally a nickname but has been adopted by Quakers themselves as common usage.

Friends World Committee for Consultation (Quakers) (FWCC)

Established in 1937 "to act in a consultative capacity to promote better understanding among Friends the world over". Around the world there are four cooperating, autonomous FWCC Sections, serving Africa, the Americas, Asia & the West Pacific, and Europe & the Middle East. FWCC's World Office is in London. Since 1948, FWCC has had 'consultative' status with the UN Economic and Social Council and is responsible for the two QUNOs.

Quaker House

Quaker House Geneva is the home of the Quaker UN Office there, housing its offices and the areas used to host lunches and other off-the-record meetings; it is also the home of the Geneva Quaker Meeting. It is a detached villa in a garden and, except for the basement meeting room, maintains its character and ambience as a house rather than an office or conference facility. Quaker House New York is a brownstone, terrace house, separate from the Quaker UN Office and is not shared with a Quaker meeting.

Quaker Peace & Social Witness (QPSW)

The body responsible for the work of British Quakers undertaken by Britain Yearly Meeting as a corporate entity. The work is supervised by committees of Quakers appointed as volunteer experts.

Quaker worship and decision-making structures

Quakers are grouped into organisations called Yearly Meetings (meeting annually), one or more within each country. Britain Yearly Meeting has a standing executive committee known as Meeting for Sufferings (so called because historically one of its functions was to record the sufferings – imprisonment – of individual Quakers). Also within Britain Yearly Meeting, and reporting to it, are area meetings (until 2007 known as monthly meetings) and, within these, local meetings (previously known as preparative meetings).

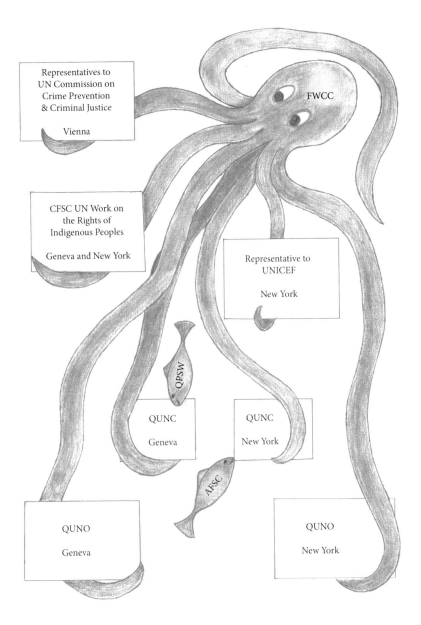

Representatives to
UN Commission on
Crime Prevention
& Criminal Justice

Vienna

FWCC

CFSC UN Work on
the Rights of
Indigenous Peoples

Geneva and New York

Representative to
UNICEF

New York

QPSW

QUNC

Geneva

QUNC

New York

AFSC

QUNO

Geneva

QUNO

New York

© Peggy Brett

QUNO

The Quaker UN Offices in Geneva and New York represent Friends worldwide and work under the auspices of the Friends World Committee for Consultation (FWCC), which has consultative status as a non-governmental organisation (NGO) with the UN Economic and Social Council. Each QUNO is small – usually in the range of three programme staff, and two to three programme assistants (one-year junior professionals). Although the names of the programmes and the specific areas of work may change, in recent years in Geneva these have broadly covered human rights and refugees, disarmament and peace, and global economic issues. In addition to the QUNOs, FWCC appoints volunteer representatives to the annual UN Commission on Crime Prevention and Criminal Justice in Vienna, and to UNICEF in New York, as well as sending delegations to various UN conferences from time to time. A different approach has been taken in relation to the UN work on the rights of indigenous peoples, with the Canadian Quakers leading on behalf of Friends worldwide, mandated by FWCC, and supported by the QUNOs. The work of each QUNO is overseen by a Quaker UN Committee (QUNC) of ten, five of whom are appointed by FWCC, and the other five by the relevant 'parent body' – Quaker Peace & Social Witness (QPSW) for Geneva and the American Friends Service Committee (AFSC) for New York.

Testimony

Quaker testimonies arise out of an inner conviction, maintained and renewed over generations by personal experience and action: they are a way rather than a form of words, although there are written versions.

UN human rights structures

The UN's main human rights[2] body is the Human Rights Council, which replaced the Commission on Human Rights in 2006. It comprises 47 government delegations elected for a fixed term and reports to the UN General Assembly, of which all UN states are members. The 'Special Procedures' of the Council are individuals or working groups appointed as independent experts to consider and report on the situation in a particular state (country mandates) or on a particular topic (thematic mandates).

In addition, when the UN adopts a human rights treaty, it normally creates a committee to supervise its implementation by states who become parties to that treaty. These 'Treaty Bodies' consist of individual experts nominated by their government (but acting in their personal capacity) and elected for a fixed term by all the states party to that treaty. Most of these Treaty Bodies can also consider complaints from individuals claiming that their rights under that particular treaty have been violated, but only if the state concerned has accepted both the treaty and the complaint procedure.

NOTES

1 Introduction

1 Much of this Introduction comes from Rachel Brett, "Living our testimonies", 19th FWCC Triennial (Birmingham, UK, 23–31 July 1997).

2 Article 71 of the UN Charter provides for such recognition of NGOs.

3 Similar reflections on the importance of being around the UN as well as using the Quaker Houses appear in Sydney Bailey, *Peace is a process*, Swarthmore Lecture (London: Quaker Home Service, 1993), pp. 147–148

2 Why Quakers work on human rights issues

1 A very similar articulation is given by Geoffrey Hubbard, *Patterns and examples: Quaker attitudes and European opportunities*, Swarthmore Lecture (London: Quaker Home Service, 1991), p. 41.

2 Adam Hochschild, *Bury the chains: The British struggle to abolish slavery* (London: Macmillan, 2005), pp. 112–113.

3 *Essays about the poor, manufactures, trade, plantations, & immorality, etc* (1699), Part 15: "Against punishing of theft and death". In George Clarke (ed), *John Bellers: his life, times and writings* (London: Routledge & Kegan Paul, 1987).

4 Tim Newell, *Forgiving justice: A Quaker vision for criminal justice*, Swarthmore Lecture (London: Quaker Home Service, 2000), p. 23.

5 From The Hamilton Declaration issued by the Friends World Committee for Consultation (FWCC) at its Triennial in 1976.

6 Elizabeth Buffum Chace, "My anti-slavery reminiscences" (1891), in Lucille Salitan and Eve Lewis Perera (eds), *Virtuous lives: Four Quaker sisters remember family life, abolitionism, and women's suffrage* (New York: Continuum, 1994), p. 115.

3 Why Quakers work at the UN

1 William Penn, *The peace of Europe, The fruits of solitude and other writings* (London: Everyman, 1993).

2 Friends Service Council, *The past is prologue: 100 years of Quaker overseas work 1868–1968* (London: FSC, 1968), p. 59.
3 Willis H. Hall, *Quaker international work in Europe since 1914* (Chambéry: Imprimeries Réunies, 1938), p. 171.
4 *Ibid.*, pp. 148–149.
5 *Ibid.*, pp. 138–141.
6 Sydney D. Bailey, *Peace is a process*, p. 88.
7 Willis H. Hall, *Quaker international work*, p. 179.
8 "Quaker Work at the United Nations" leaflet (undated).
9 Friends Service Council, *The past is prologue*, p. 59.
10 Carolyn Hayman, *Ripples into waves: Locally led peacebuilding on a national scale* (Peace Direct and QUNO, 2010).

4 Why the particular human rights issues that QUNO takes up

1 Abbreviated from the *Australian Friend* (December 2010).
2 See Rachel Brett, "Implementing a prophetic vision through international law", in Brian Phillips and John Lampen (eds), *Endeavours to mend: A British Quaker perspective on witness in the world today* (London: Quaker Books, 2006).
3 Nicolas Hulot and Sipa-Press, *Ces Enfants qui souffrent* (Paris: PAC, 1978).
4 Peter Townsend, *The smallest pawns in the game* (London: Granada, 1980).
5 Dorothea E. Woods, "Children bearing and using military arms", unpublished paper (January 1980).
6 See on this and more generally for the Quaker history and approach to criminal justice, Tim Newell, *Forgiving justice: A Quaker vision for criminal justice*, in particular pp. 17–29.
7 Letter to the author from Susan Hartshorne, 10 August 2009.
8 This group was subsequently renamed the Crime, Community and Justice Group.
9 Minute 21/21, 21st FWCC Triennial, 16–25 January 2004, King's College, Auckland, Aotearoa/New Zealand.
10 In fact, a specific Women in Prison Project Group was established with four Quaker agencies involved: FWCC Vienna representation; QUNO Geneva; QPSW Crime, Community

and Justice group; and the Quaker Council on European Affairs (QCEA) to bring in the European dimension.

11 Extract from Yearly Meeting Epistle in *Christian Faith & Practice* (1959 edn), para. 574.

12 FWCC oral statement to the UN Sub-Commission on the Prevention of Discrimination and Protection of Minorities, 14 August 1984.

13 See Rachel Brett, "Persistent objectors at the United Nations" in *The Friends Quarterly*, 35.7 (July 2007), pp. 301–309.

14 Willis H. Hall, *Quaker international work in Europe since 1914*, pp. 52–53.

15 *Ibid.*, p. 61.

16 Sydney Bailey, *Peace is a process*, p. 113.

17 C. H. Mike Yarrow, *Quaker experiences in international conciliation* (New Haven: Yale University Press, 1978), p. 44.

18 Sydney Bailey, *Peace is a process*, p. 113.

19 At the 1985 FWCC Triennial in Mexico, Friends were asked to contribute through FWCC to the UN Voluntary Fund for the Victims of Torture, and regular contributions were made to the fund at least until 1988.

20 Elaine Bishop states: "I have personally been told by an Indigenous Person from New York state that his people trust Quakers because Quakers kept their word with First Nations." (Text presented to Canadian Yearly Meeting during the 1999 sessions by Elaine Bishop as part of the [Canadian] Quaker Aboriginal Affairs Committee/CFSC evening.)

21 20th FWCC Triennial, New Hampshire, USA, 22–30 July 2000.

22 Thomas G. Weiss and David A. Korn, *Internal displacement: Conceptualization and its consequences* (London: Routledge, 2006), pp. 19–23.

23 Identification by Rachel Brett, work undertaken by Tim Wichert, who was seconded to QUNO by the Mennonite Central Committee for three years to work on refugee issues.

5 How Quakers work at the UN

1 The WTO is not a UN body but a multilateral institution based in Geneva and has been an important focus of the trade and economics work of QUNO.

2 Africa; Asia; Latin America and Caribbean; Western Europe and Other; Central and Eastern Europe.

3 The then main regular UN political human rights forum – that is, made up of representatives of governments. Now replaced by the UN Human Rights Council.

4 Tony Stoller, *Wrestling with the angel*, Swarthmore Lecture (London: Quaker Books, 2001), pp. 64–65.

5 Gunnar Sundberg, "United Quaker Service", paper for the Annual Meeting of the European Section of FWCC at Charbonnières, France, Easter 1963.

6 The Committee is mandated to hold an annual Day of General Discussion. The purpose of the Days of General Discussion is to foster a deeper understanding of the contents and implications of the Convention as they relate to specific articles or topics. Representatives of governments, UN human rights mechanisms, UN bodies and specialised agencies, non-governmental organizations, national human rights institutions as well as individual experts and children are welcome to take part.

7 Now Child Soldiers International.

8 This is well set out by Adam Curle, *True justice*, Swarthmore Lecture (London: Quaker Home Service, 1981), pp. 81–82.

9 See Wolf Mendl, *Prophets and reconcilers*, Swarthmore Lecture (London: Friends Home Service Committee, 1974), who cites John Woolman as one of the "rare few" who "seem to combine both and achieve a triumphant witness which is a beacon to those who come after", p. 9.

10 Sydney Bailey, *Peace is a process*, p. 7.

11 A related though different issue is the question of taking up individual cases, for which Sydney Bailey articulated a 3-part test: (1) Is the action complained of an infraction of some international obligation of the country concerned, such as a violation of a human rights treaty? (2) Is the victim known personally to Quaker workers? (3) Are we sure of the relevant

facts? (Peace is a process, p. 116). These days, in practice there are so many possible human rights procedures which the individual or their family or contacts can use, that we tend anyway to advise on the available avenues and how to use them rather than taking up cases ourselves.

12 J. Duncan Wood, *The background to Quaker work at the United Nations* (Quaker Peace & Service, 1987).

13 Published as: Rachel Brett and Margaret McCallin, *Children:The invisible soldiers* (Stockholm: Rädda Barnen, 1996; 2nd edn 1998).

14 Rachel Brett and Irma Specht, *Young soldiers: Why they choose to fight* (London: ILO/Lynne Rienner, 2004). QUNO New York also published Yvonne E. Keairns, *The voice of girl child soldiers* (2002).

15 UN General Assembly resolution 33/165 of December 1978 (commonly known as the CO/apartheid resolution). I had just started my internship at QUNO New York and worked with Gordon M. Browne Jr on this, including preparing the draft resolution.

16 For more detail see Rachel Brett and Laurel Townhead, "Conscientious objection to military service" in G. Gilbert, F. Hampson and C. Sandoval (eds), *Strategic visions for human rights: Essays in honour of Professor Kevin Boyle* (London: Routledge, 2011); and Rachel Brett, "Persistent objectors at the United Nations" in *The Friends Quarterly*, 35.7 (July 2007), pp. 301–309.

17 *Yeo-Bum Yoon and Myung-Jin Choi v Republic of Korea*, CCPR/C/88/D/1321-1322/2004, 1 December 2006.

18 *Bayatyan v Armenia* (application no. 23459/03), 7 July 2011

19 The Human Security Network (HSN) was launched at the initiative of Canada and Norway in the margins of the UN General Assembly in 1998 as an informal group of countries with the goal of encouraging resolution of international issues that present an immediate threat to human security. The original intention was to promote the Ottawa Convention (banning anti-personnel mines), but this later expanded to other international issues endangering human security, including the

protection of children in armed conflicts. Twelve countries take part: Austria, Chile, Greece, Ireland, Jordan, Canada, Costa Rica, Mali, Norway, Slovenia, Switzerland and Thailand, with South Africa as an observer.

20 Stoller, *Wrestling with the angel*, p. 86. I was intrigued to see this reference, having used exactly the same analogy myself in the above context.

21 UNHCR Executive Committee, *Conclusion on refugees with disabilities and other persons with disabilities protected and assisted by UNHCR*, No. 110 (LXI) – 2010.

22 Falstaff in William Shakespeare's *Henry IV, Part 2*: "I am not only witty in myself, but the cause that wit is in other men."

23 Evaluanda, *External Evaluation Project "Women in Prison and Children of Imprisoned Mothers" funded by Irish Aid (2008– 2011)*, Quaker United Nations Office, Geneva (Final report, May 2011).

24 Duncan and Katharine Wood, "Notes on the activities of the Geneva Centre", Geneva, 22 January 1964.

25 Evaluanda, *External evaluation project "Women in prison and children of imprisoned mothers"*.

26 Duncan and Katharine Wood, "Notes on the activities of the Geneva Centre", Geneva, 22 January 1964.

27 The Durban Review Conference took place in April 2009 to evaluate progress towards the goals set by the World Conference against Racism, Racial Discrimination, Xenophobia and Related Intolerance held in Durban, South Africa, in 2001, about which various controversies arose, including a walkout by some governments.

28 Geneva Centre, *Newsletter*, 9.4 (May 1973), Annex p. ix.

29 Quaker House Geneva, *Newsletter*, 10.4 (August 1977), p. 33.

30 Rachel Taylor, *Women in prison and children of imprisoned mothers: Preliminary research paper* (Geneva: QUNO, July 2004).

31 As of June 2011, 87 countries from all five UN regions have issued standing invitations to Special Procedures.

6 Conclusion

1   See Constance Braithwaite, *Conscientious objection to compulsions under the law* (York: William Sessions, 1995).
2   UN Commission on Human Rights resolution 1998/77.
3   Example quoted by Sydney Bailey, *Peace is a process*, p. 28.
4   "Military conscription: A statement by the Religious Society of Friends (Quakers)" (May 1945).
5   Duncan and Katharine Wood, "Epilogue", Quaker House Geneva, *Newsletter*, 10.4 (August 1977), p. 38.

Glossary

1   Christine A. M. Davis, *Minding the future*, Swarthmore Lecture (London: Quaker Books, 2008), p. 50.
2   An excellent introduction to human rights is: Andrew Clapham, *Human rights: A very short introduction* (Oxford: Oxford University Press, 2007).

BIBLIOGRAPHY

Bailey, Sydney, *Peace is a Process*, Swarthmore Lecture (London: Quaker Home Service, 1993)

Bellers, John, *Essays about the poor, manufactures, trade, plantations, & immorality, etc* (1699) in George Clarke (ed), John Bellers: his life, times and writings (London: Routledge & Kegan Paul, 1987)

Braithwaite, Constance, *Conscientious objection to compulsions under the law* (York: William Sessions, 1995)

Brett, Rachel, "Living our testimonies", 19th FWCC Triennial (Birmingham, UK, 23–31 July 1997)

Brett, Rachel, and Margaret McCallin, *Children: The invisible soldiers* (Stockholm: Rädda Barnen, 1996; 2nd edn 1998)

Brett, Rachel, and Irma Specht, *Young soldiers: Why they choose to fight* (London: ILO/Lynne Rienner, 2004)

Brett, Rachel, "Implementing a prophetic vision through international law", in Brian Phillips and John Lampen (eds), *Endeavours to mend: A British Quaker perspective on witness in the world today* (London: Quaker Books, 2006)

Brett, Rachel, "Persistent objectors at the United Nations" in *The Friends Quarterly*, 35.7 (July 2007)

Brett, Rachel, and Laurel Townhead, "Conscientious objection to military service" in G. Gilbert, F. Hampson and C. Sandoval (eds), *Strategic visions for human rights: Essays in honour of Professor Kevin Boyle* (London: Routledge, 2011)

Clapham, Andrew, *Human rights: A very short introduction* (Oxford: Oxford University Press, 2007)

Curle, Adam, *True justice*, Swarthmore Lecture (London: Quaker Home Service, 1981)

Davis, Christine A. M., *Minding the future*, Swarthmore Lecture (London: Quaker Books, 2008)

Friends Service Council, *The past is prologue: 100 years of Quaker overseas work 1868–1968* (London: FSC, 1968)

Hall, Willis H., *Quaker international work in Europe since 1914* (Chambéry: Imprimeries Réunies, 1938)

Hayman, Carolyn, *Ripples into waves: Locally led peacebuilding on a national scale* (Peace Direct and QUNO, 2010)

Hochschild, Adam, *Bury the chains: The British struggle to abolish slavery* (London: Macmillan, 2005)

Hubbard, Geoffrey, *Patterns and examples: Quaker attitudes and European opportunities*, Swarthmore Lecture (London: Quaker Home Service, 1991)

Hulot, Nicolas, and Sipa-Press, *Ces Enfants qui souffrent* (Paris: PAC, 1978)

Keairns, Yvonne E., *The voice of girl child soldiers* (2002)

Mendl, Wolf, *Prophets and reconcilers*, Swarthmore Lecture (London: Friends Home Service Committee, 1974)

Newell, Tim, *Forgiving justice: A Quaker vision for criminal justice*, Swarthmore Lecture (London: Quaker Home Service, 2000)

Penn, William, *The peace of Europe, The fruits of solitude and other writings* (London: Everyman, 1993)

Salitan, Lucille, and Eve Lewis Perera (eds), *Virtuous lives: Four Quaker sisters remember family life, abolitionism, and women's suffrage* (New York: Continuum, 1994)

Stoller, Tony, *Wrestling with the angel*, Swarthmore Lecture (London: Quaker Books, 2001)

Taylor, Rachel, *Women in prison and children of imprisoned mothers: Preliminary research paper* (Geneva: QUNO, July 2004)

Townsend, Peter, *The smallest pawns in the game* (London: Granada, 1980)

Weiss, Thomas G., and David A. Korn, *Internal displacement: Conceptualization and its consequences* (London: Routledge, 2006)

Wood, J. Duncan, *The background to the work at the United Nations* (London: Quaker Peace & Service, 1987)

Yarrow, C. H. Mike, *Quaker experiences in international conciliation* (New Haven: Yale University Press, 1978)